THE LAST
BOARDING PARTY

The USMC and the SS *Mayaguez* 1975

CLAYTON K.S. CHUN

``First published in Great Britain in 2011 by Osprey Publishing, Midland House, West Way, Botley, Oxford, OX2 0PH, UK

44–02 23rd St, Suite 219, Long Island City, NY 11101, USA

E-mail: info@ospreypublishing.com

A CIP catalogue record for this book is available from the British Library

Print ISBN: 978 1 84908 425 3
PDF e-book ISBN: 9781849084260

Page layout by Bounford.com, Cambridge, UK
Index by David Worthington
Typeset in Sabon
Maps by Bounford.com
BEVs by Alan Gilliland
Originated by United Graphics Pte, Singapore
Printed in China through Worldprint

11 12 13 14 15   10 9 8 7 6 5 4 3 2 1

Osprey Publishing is supporting the Woodland Trust, the UK's leading woodland conservation charity, by funding the dedication of trees.

www.ospreypublishing.com

ACKNOWLEDGMENTS

I would like to thank Colonel (ret.) Walt Wood, USMC, from the US Army War College, for the use of his photographs. Additionally, Dr George Watson, Air Force History Office, provided me with some additional perspectives on the mission and helped me secure some of the USAF photographs. Mr Mike Semrau, US Army War College, was kind enough to get me a copy of video from the *Mayaguez* incident. Lastly, I appreciate the encouragement from Philip Smith from Osprey Publishing in completing this project.

GLOSSARY

7AF	7th Air Force
13AF	13th Air Force
ABCCC	airborne battlefield communications, command, and control
ARRS	Aerospace Rescue and Recovery Squadron
ARRW	Aerospace Rescue and Recovery Wing
BDA	bomb damage assessment
BLT	battalion landing team
CBU	cluster bomb unit
CIA	Central Intelligence Agency
CINCPAC	Commander-in-Chief, Pacific
CINCPACAF	Commander-in-Chief, Pacific Air Forces
CINCPACFLT	Commander-in-Chief, Pacific Fleet
COMUSSAG	Commander, US Support Activities Group
DCI	Director of Central Intelligence
DIA	Defense Intelligence Agency
DoD	Department of Defense
EOD	explosive ordnance disposal
FAC	forward air controller
IPAC	Intelligence Pacific
JCS	Joint Chiefs of Staff
JG	Jolly Green
K	Knife
MSC	Military Sealift Command
NMCC	National Military Command Center
NSA	National Security Agency
NSC	National Security Council
NVA	North Vietnamese Army
PACFLT	Pacific Fleet
PGM	precision guided munition
POL	petroleum, oil, and lubricant
RCA	riot control agent
RPG	rocket-propelled grenade
SAC	Strategic Air Command
SOS	Special Operations Squadron
SOW	Special Operations Wing
SW	Strategic Wing
TASS	Tactical Air Support Squadron
TFS	Tactical Fighter Squadron
TFW	Tactical Fighter Wing
TOT	time over target
USAF	US Air Force
USSAG	US Support Activities Group
UHF	ultra high frequency

CONTENTS

INTRODUCTION

The Vietnam War was one of the most divisive conflicts in American history. After more than a decade of involvement in South Vietnam, Washington negotiated a peace with Hanoi in 1973. US combat operations officially ended on January 28, 1973, when a ceasefire took effect. The United States' military disengagement in other Southeast Asian nations, however, would take longer. Washington officially stopped bombing in Laos on February 21, but continued authorizing sorties until April 17. On August 15, the last military combat sorties over Cambodian skies concluded the US war. Yet despite massive aid and some political support by Washington, Saigon still fell in 1975. Laos and Cambodia turned into communist states.

These actions seemed to confirm fears of a regional communist takeover, apparently proving the "domino theory" first advanced in the 1950s. One of the few Southeast Asian nations that seemed to escape revolution was Thailand, but its government was nevertheless changing. Although a shadow of its former self, the only sizeable American military presence in the region was in Thailand and the Philippines. Despite a calm exterior, elements within Bangkok wanted to expel the US Air Force (USAF) units stationed throughout the country.

Southeast Asia in turmoil

During the Vietnam War, North Vietnam had largely moved from an insurgency to a conventional war to overthrow the Saigon government by 1975, and now had designs on other neighboring states. The Laotian and Cambodian governments, meanwhile, faced counter-revolutionary movements. Both governments had been, at times, willing to accept American aid in exchange for their support in fighting a secret war against the North Vietnamese Army (NVA) and Viet Cong (VC). With Washington pulling out of South Vietnam, however, the administrations started to crumble. The Laotian leadership, without massive American aid and bombing support, suffered continuing setbacks against communist Pathet Lao and NVA units bent on the government's overthrow. Laos was valuable to the North Vietnamese as an indirect route to South Vietnam. A ceasefire on February 22, 1973, allowed the communists to control wide areas of the countryside, and although a coalition government was formed under Prince Souvanna Phouma, the Pathet Lao continued to consolidate its power. Eventually Laos fell to the communists in December 1975.

In Cambodia, Defense Minister General Lon Nol, sympathetic to American foreign and military aims, had clashed with head of state Prince Norodom Sihanouk over national policies, including the prince's complaints about American and South Vietnamese border incursions, bombings, and aid. US and South Vietnamese forces had briefly invaded Cambodia in late April 1970 to oust Vietnamese troops and destroy supplies in the border area with South Vietnam. These differences strained relations between Washington and Phnom Penh, and in 1970 Lon Nol launched a coup, forcing Sihanouk to abdicate. His assumption of power sparked a war with the Khmer Rouge, Cambodian communists supported by the North Vietnamese and Chinese. He would eventually leave office, but later return to power in 1972, when he suspended the constitution. Lon Nol announced a ceasefire on January 29, 1973, but it never took hold. Khmer Rouge, NVA, and VC forces controlled rural Cambodia, and they had bottled up Lon Nol's forces in the cities.

Phnom Penh relied heavily on American airpower and support to survive. Khmer Rouge forces, with support from Sihanouk, continued to fight on. They started to surround Phnom Penh, shutting down the Mekong River access and shelling and rocketing Pochentong Airport, the major airfield near Phnom Penh. Despite American air-delivered aid, it was not enough to stem the tide. Lon Nol abdicated and left for Hawaii, and the Khmer Rouge took over the country in April 1975.

The leader of the Khmer Rouge, Pol Pot, did not allow Sihanouk to return to power. Instead, he began a process aimed at rebuilding Cambodia into a self-reliant, agrarian state. He also carried out mass executions among the nation's business owners, political opposition, government employees, Buddhist monks, and various ethnic groups, including Vietnamese and Chinese. Pol Pot also continued the border disputes with Vietnam and Thailand to demonstrate his resolve for maintaining Cambodian sovereignty. Cambodian military forces began to occupy disputed islands in the Gulf of Thailand. The Khmer Rouge also wanted to extend their territory to offshore waters. Foreign embassies and citizens were not immune to this onslaught. Pol Pot's regime told foreigners to leave and, in some cases, forcibly removed them from Cambodia. These actions not only demonstrated Pol Pot's xenophobic nature, but a vicious character.

American National Security Agency (NSA) signal intercepts became the most reliable information source available on Khmer Rouge activities. President Gerald Ford's administration started receiving NSA signals intelligence, that indicated that the Khmer Rouge had initiated mass executions, re-education efforts, forced relocations, retribution actions, and family separations "on an unbelievable scale." Within the White House, speculation ran rampant on why the new Cambodian government had taken these paths.

JANUARY 28 1973

end of US combat ops in Vietnam

Future relations between Phnom Penh, Washington and other nations seemed bleak. Cambodia's aggressive border behavior and willingness to execute its own people had the potential to cause more conflict within Southeast Asia. Fortunately, for Washington, the United States had largely withdrawn from the region. The only major American military presence in mainland Southeast Asia was in Thailand.

The Thai government had allowed American airpower to conduct bomber, fighter, reconnaissance, and tanker operations throughout the region virtually unconstrained. Bangkok stood by for years as F-105s and later B-52s and F-111s hammered Hanoi. This situation was changing, however. Communist revolutionary forces had tumbled Vietnam, Laos, and Cambodia, so Thailand could be next. Bangkok did not want to upset her neighbors unduly and bring a communist insurgency within Thailand. The United States had several air

THE FALL OF SOUTH VIETNAM AND OPERATION *FREQUENT WIND*

The United States had removed all of its combat units from the Republic of Vietnam well before 1975. Although Washington had supported Saigon with equipment and money, the US Congress had reduced aid to South Vietnam as the nation focused on other issues. Hanoi still looked south as it saw the American public's interest in Southeast Asia rapidly waning. North Vietnamese and VC forces had already failed to conquer South Vietnam during the 1968 Tet Offensive, and Saigon turned back Hanoi's conventional invasion in the 1972 Easter Offensive. By 1975, however, Saigon could not rely on massive American airpower or military resupply to stem another northern invasion. North Vietnamese divisions streamed south and pushed aside South Vietnamese units. Ford tried to get a $300 million aid package to Saigon, but the Congress refused to pass it. The Republic of Vietnam's days were numbered.

Phouc Binh, a provincial capital, fell on January 6, 1975. North Vietnam took Ban Me Thuot, a key city in the central highlands, in March. South Vietnamese Army units fled to the coast. South Vietnam's President Nguyen Van Thieu decided to abandon much of the highlands and concentrate on defending major cities, but Hue fell on March 26. Two days later, NVA forces took South Vietnam's second largest city, Da Nang. Saigon was next.

Events escalated. On April 1, Cambodian President Lon Nol exited the country, and American forces executed Operation *Eagle Pull* to extract all American personnel from Phnom Penh on April 16. Some South Vietnamese forces started to switch sides; two South Vietnamese Air

Force F-5Es dropped bombs on the Presidential Palace on April 8. South Vietnamese Army units deserted and threw away their uniforms as the North Vietnamese surrounded Saigon. Thieu resigned on April 21. A week later, the American embassy prepared landing zones for the coming helicopter evacuation.

South Vietnamese citizens had already started leaving the country by boat and plane well before April. The US government had helped 160,000 refugees flee the country. Many of these refugees fled by boat and entered camps throughout Asia. Tens of thousands of them eventually entered the United States. In early April, USAF C-5As had started Operation *Baby Lift* to transport infants, some of them orphans, out of the country. One C-5A crashed, killing 206 people, 172 of whom were children. Some alleged that a North Vietnamese SA-7 shot down the plane.

American Navy, Marine Corps, and USAF helicopters started the evacuation from the American embassy on April 28 under Operation *Frequent Wind*. USAF C-141 and C-130 aircraft also took people out of the country from Tan Son Nhut Air Base. Three South Vietnamese Air Force A-37s attacked the airfield and flew north. UH-1, CH-53, HH-53, and CH-46 helicopters, some participants of the Cambodian evacuation, pulled out 1,373 Americans, 6,422 foreign nationals, and the 989-strong marine security detachment. Two marines died and losses included three aircraft during the operation. On April 29, the end came. The last Americans destroyed equipment and documents at Tan Son Nhut and Ambassador Graham Martin left the embassy that day.

bases that maintained strategic bombers, tactical fighters, and special operations aircraft and helicopters. Although Washington did not have major ground forces in Thailand, its air and naval forces had the capability to conduct limited attacks on Vietnam, Laos, or Cambodia.

Thailand was also concerned about border incursions. Disputes about border locations, the ownership of islands, or land areas had plagued Southeast Asia for decades. Criminal activities took advantage of these disputes to operate drug smuggling or piracy operations. The VC and NVA had used the borders between Vietnam, Laos, and Cambodia to operate the Ho Chi Minh trail, transporting supplies, arms, and troops into South Vietnam. By 1975, opposing sides moves across borders to support regional revolutionary and counter-revolutionary movements. Counter-revolutionary forces, for example, operated in southern and northeastern Thailand against the Khmer Rouge. Their activities spawned small cross-border attacks by Cambodia, supported by Vietnam and China. Another issue heightening tensions was the flood of refugees streaming across the Thai border.

America charts a new path

In the second half of the 1970s, the United States was trying to forget about Vietnam and move on. Washington had started advising the South Vietnamese in 1961, but left after years of combat that resulted in 58,193 American deaths. By early 1975, observers witnessed South Vietnamese defenses crumble as the North Vietnamese pushed south. Without American military firepower and aid, Saigon was ready to fall. America had "lost" its first war, which ended with a massive helicopter and ship evacuation that put a stain on national honor.

The American public would not support any move to stem further communist expansion in Southeast Asia. To limit further American involvement in the region, the Congress started to restrain the power of the presidency. The Cooper-Church Amendment, passed in the Senate on June 19, 1973, restricted the nation from providing any funds to finance American military operations in Southeast Asia, unless authorized by Congress. This amendment undermined any perception that the United States would aid South Vietnam or other nation if it came under attack by a communist movement.

The Vietnam War had taken place in the context of a wider conflict, the Cold War. Since the end of World War II, the United States and the free world were in a state of continual conflict with the Soviet Union and the Warsaw Pact. The Nixon administration had tried to defuse tensions with its communist rivals, yet the United States still faced a huge arsenal of nuclear weapons aimed at it. The North Atlantic Treaty Organization (NATO) faced the Soviet military on the German border. Armed proxies

President Gerald Ford assumed the presidency after Richard Nixon's resignation. The *Mayaguez* incident was his first foreign policy crisis. Ford was anxious to avoid a long negotiated settlement if Phnom Penh decided to hold the crew hostage. He wanted a swift resolution that included possible military action. (US Air Force)

**APRIL 1
1975**

**Cambodian
president Lon Nol
flees country**

waged a war representing East and West, and Soviet-backed Arab states fought American-armed Israel. Marxist-led revolutionary movements sprouted throughout Latin America, Asia, and Africa. One of the hottest spots in the world was the border between North and South Korea, two countries technically still at war. Fortunately, the People's Republic of China (PRC) and America were trying to normalize relations after years of silence. Yet Washington was still unsure of its future path. American military forces around the world stood on alert to respond to any conflict, from an insurgency to global nuclear war. Demonstrating American military power was deemed as crucial to deter any future enemies.

The US government faced another challenge. Years of civil strife and protests over the Vietnam War had changed America's outlook on the world. Within a few years, the optimism of the Kennedy administration's internationalism disintegrated into insularity. Congress and the public were skeptical of any foreign adventure. Gerald Ford had inherited a country that was cynical about the government, especially after revelations about the Tonkin Gulf incident, the release of the Pentagon Papers, Watergate, and other issues. Given the mood of the nation, other powers wondered if Washington could act decisively.

A powder keg in the Gulf of Thailand

The Gulf of Thailand did not seem to be an area of potential conflict to most Americans. After all, the reason for the war in Southeast Asia – saving the Republic of Vietnam – no longer existed. Trade ships plied the tranquil waters, but a new government, old rivalries, and plenty of weapons did not mix well. Under Lon Nol, the United States provided not only bombing sorties against the Khmer Rouge, but massive military and economic aid. After Cambodia's fall, the communist insurgents now had access to American military supplies in the form of aircraft, small arms, and naval craft. Pol Pot had the ability to expand his power across Cambodia's borders. The Khmer Rouge had the will and ability to launch a wide range of outrages. The Americans had left the region and it appeared they would not return for any reason; American military forces had returned to a training status throughout the Pacific.

Ship seizures, however, began to occur throughout the Gulf of Thailand, as Cambodian communists started to exert their new power in the region. The White House and other government agencies did not receive reports of any American ships attacked, however, so the government agencies did not issue immediate mariners' warnings to the public or interested parties. Yet the attacks were growing in frequency, and included international commercial ships.

The seeming end of the Vietnam War in May 1975 was an illusion. A return to conflict in Southeast Asia began on a sunny afternoon south of the Cambodian mainland. Soon, world newspapers announced the capture and detainment of an American container ship. Inevitably, American military actions swiftly followed.

ORIGINS

Long-simmering territorial disputes, control of potential oil deposits, and concerns about American-supported insurgents had pushed the new communist government in Phnom Penh to defend its oceanic sovereignty around Cambodia. Nations in the region had a history of geographical disputes that made relations contentious for decades. Some of these issues arose after France withdrew from her colonies in Indochina, resulting in the independence of Cambodia, Laos, and South Vietnam. For several years, Phnom Penh sparred over borders shared with South Vietnam, Thailand, and Laos. In the Gulf of Thailand, ongoing questions regarding undefined maritime boundaries and ownership of several islands led to problems, including armed confrontations between South Vietnam and Thailand.

Pol Pot's rise to power did not alter Cambodia's border problems. Khmer Rouge forces, despite recently taking control of Cambodia, were still trying to assert sovereignty over several islands, including Poulo Wai, Hon Panjang, and Dao Phu Quoc. Cambodian soldiers had raided Dao Phu Quoc, for example, on May 1, 1975, to demonstrate the government's seriousness over this issue. The boundary problems were not only about national honor, but also control over a more substantive resource – petroleum. These islands contained potential oil reserves that might bring wealth to a war-ravaged nation. Whatever country controlled this area would have a great advantage to get access to oil and natural gas reserves.

Revolution in Cambodia cemented apparent communist control over the country. Although the Khmer Rouge had secured the nation, the fight had been long and bloody. The former Lon Nol government had received vast quantities of arms and funds from the United States, while the vehement xenophobia of Pol Pot's government contributed to a heightened fear of potential foreign activities to overthrow the new communist regime. Khmer Rouge military units were on alert to intercept Central Intelligence Agency (CIA) funded insurgents crossing the border with Thailand, or landing from ships transiting the Gulf of Thailand. Pol Pot was still fearful that merchant ships, in the guise of commercial trade, were secretly funneling CIA weapons

**APRIL 16
1975**

**US personnel
evacuated from
Phnom Penh**

This *Mayaguez* photograph shows the container ship after its recovery. The ship was *en route* from Hong Kong to Singapore with a stop in Thailand when it was captured. After the incident, it continued to serve as a freighter until its owners scrapped it in 1979. (US Navy)

to insurgents trying to ignite a counter-revolution. Additionally, the Cambodian government was also concerned about potential American espionage efforts to aid its enemies. The new government had started to expel all foreigners from Cambodian soil, and foreign governments could not contact the Pol Pot government directly. Compounding this problem was the new regime's struggles to organize the government and get control over its military forces and foreign relations, activities that needed time to consolidate.

Boundary squabbles and perceived security questions were immediate problems that required solutions. One method to illustrate Cambodian resolve was to maintain a naval presence and demonstrate aggressively its ability to enforce its maritime boundaries. Khmer Rouge Swift boats, former US Navy patrol craft captured from the Lon Nol government, provided the capability to enforce Cambodian boundary claims. In early May 1975, Khmer Rouge naval units started to seize vessels in the Gulf of Thailand. On May 2, Cambodian military forces took control of seven Thai fishing boats. Two days later, the South Korean freighter *Masan Ho* avoided seizure, but Khmer Rouge gunboats chased and fired upon the ship. Khmer Rouge naval units also took refugee boats fleeing South Vietnam. The most serious maritime incident occurred on May 7, when Cambodians held a Panamanian freighter for 35 hours. Phnom Penh officials had ordered the detention and interrogation of the ship and crew. The communist government's actions were not new; under Lon Nol, Cambodian naval forces had also taken Thai fishing boats caught in its waters.

Cambodians were not the only military forces in the region. Khmer Rouge naval forces had witnessed American military and commercial shipping throughout the Gulf of Thailand area. Washington maintained several USAF tactical and strategic wings on bases in Thailand, remnants of the massive American Southeast Asian military presence to fight the Vietnam War. USAF aircraft flew training missions throughout the region, and the US Navy had evacuated American citizens and others when Phnom Penh fell to the communists. US Pacific Fleet (PACFLT) ships patrolled the Gulf of Thailand to aid refugees fleeing both Cambodia and Vietnam. Additionally P-3 Orion antisubmarine aircraft conducted surveillance missions that included flying near Cambodia.

The end of the Vietnam War did not stop the Cold War. Washington still had to contend with Soviet Pacific naval activities along with securing trade routes for American and allied nations. PACFLT assets also conducted training exercises and transited international waters. However, disagreements arose about what constituted international waters. Washington insisted on recognizing only a 3 nautical mile territorial boundary while Phnom Penh, among other Southeast Asian states, claimed a 12 nautical mile limit. Cambodia had argued for such a boundary since 1969. Despite these incidents, commercial shipping continued to travel to routine destinations through the region.

"Mayday"

One of the hundreds of commercial vessels plying the Pacific trading routes was the SS *Mayaguez*. The *Mayaguez* was a 10,485-ton containerized American-flagged cargo ship. Built in 1944 as the SS *White Falcon*, the ship had a crew of 40 and carried 107 commercial, 77 military, and 90 empty containers on May 12. Charles T. Miller was *Mayaguez*'s captain and the voyage initially seemed uneventful. He was guiding the ship from Hong Kong via Sattahip, Thailand, to its final destination of Singapore. Miller would drop off the military cargo at Sattahip. This cargo did not include weapons; instead, it contained machine parts, supplies, mail, replacement equipment, commissary goods, and food. The remaining military containers, about half of the cargo, was destined for base exchanges at the USAF's Thai installations. The *Mayaguez*'s path would pass close to Poulo Wai. Khmer Rouge units had already taken the island from the Vietnamese. Despite the recent ship seizures, Miller had not received any warnings about problems with Khmer Rouge gunboats. The vessel steamed at 12.5 knots on a heading towards Thailand.

At 1418hrs on May 12, two Cambodian Swift boats approached the *Mayaguez* and fired across the bow and down her sides with rockets and .50-caliber rounds. Fortunately, the *Mayaguez*'s radio operator transmitted a Mayday message that reported they were under attack. Miller was about 7 nautical miles southwest of Poulo Wai when seven Khmer Rouge naval

The National Security Council met several times during the *Mayaguez* incident. Ford's administration had several Nixon appointees who gave him an experienced national security team. Here acting Chairman of the Joint Chiefs of Staff, General David C. Jones, briefs Ford as William Colby, Director of Central Intelligence, looks on. (Ford Presidential Library)

**APRIL 17
1975**

**Pol Pot takes
Phnom Penh**

personnel boarded his ship. Poluo Wai is located approximately 60 nautical miles south of the Cambodian mainland. Armed with a combination of AK-47 and rocket-propelled grenade (RPG) weapons, the Khmer Rouge boarding party indicated, on navigational maps, for Miller to proceed to Kompong Som. Kompong Som, is a port complex on the Cambodian coast. However, the *Mayaguez* had a damaged radar system that could endanger the vessel, since there were many shallow reefs in the region, which would be especially difficult to negotiate if Miller proceeded to Kompong Som at night.

John Neal of the Delta Exploration Company, in Jakarta, Indonesia, received the following emergency message: "Have been fired upon and boarded by Cambodian armed forces at 9 degrees 48 minutes North/102 degrees 53 minutes East. Ship being towed to unknown Cambodian port." Neal tried to raise the *Mayaguez*, but failed to do so. He then contacted the American embassy in Jakarta to report the incident. Another shipping agency in Singapore also transmitted the message to the local American embassy. Washington would soon hear about the boarding. The US defense attaché in Singapore notified PACFLT's Commander, Seventh Fleet. The American ambassador in Jakarta sent immediate messages to the White House, NSA, CIA, Defense Intelligence Agency (DIA), National Military Command Center (NMCC) at the Pentagon, Commander-in-Chief, Pacific (CINCPAC), and other appropriate commands. CINCPAC was the regional combatant command responsible for military actions in the Pacific area, including the Gulf of Thailand. Located in Honolulu, Hawaii, CINCPAC only had command of assigned air, naval, ground, and marine forces. Other forces in-theater, such as strategic reconnaissance aircraft, belonged to other commands. NMCC officials started to discuss the *Mayaguez* situation with the CINCPAC staff and suggested that they prepare to send Navy and USAF reconnaissance aircraft to search for and locate the *Mayaguez*.

Acting Chairman of the Joint Chiefs of Staff (JCS), General David C. Jones, received the news about the *Mayaguez* at 0646hrs. In Cambodia the local time was 1746hrs, and time zone differences would affect some coordination and decision-making. About 45 minutes later, Jones ordered CINCPAC to launch reconnaissance aircraft to locate the *Mayaguez*. Fortunately, search aircraft would have to go no further than Poulo Wai; due to approaching darkness and the broken radar, Miller convinced his Cambodian captors to anchor off the island.

President Gerald R. Ford had been in office less than a year. Ford had replaced Richard M. Nixon, who had resigned in lieu of facing impeachment due to the Watergate scandal. At his 0740hrs daily intelligence briefing, CIA briefers told Ford about the *Mayaguez*. Washington would soon react.

**MAY
1975**

**Khmer Rouge
naval units start
seizing vessels in
the Gulf of
Thailand**

INITIAL STRATEGY

Pol Pot's government had no qualms about severing contacts with foreign powers, especially the United States. As we have seen, Lon Nol had received extensive American military aid, to include air support, for use against the Khmer Rouge. By April 1975, Washington had evacuated all military and government personnel from South Vietnam, withdrew from Cambodia, and had been humiliated worldwide with the rise of communist movements throughout Southeast Asia. Although the United States suffered greatly from the fall of Saigon on April 30, 1975, it still had air and naval theater forces capable of attacking Cambodia. Why would Phnom Penh tempt an attack by a superpower by seizing an American ship?

Great speculation surrounds why Cambodians seized the *Mayaguez*. Cambodians had previously detained foreign shipping in their territorial waters. The *Mayaguez* boarding may have been an extension of previous Cambodian government activities, but those policies focused on small fishing boats, not major international shipping. Phnom Penh's attempt to maintain its sovereignty while interdicting potential counter-revolutionaries and arms might have given more motivation for ship seizures. Conversely, the Cambodians may have sought a way to blackmail or embarrass Washington by capturing the ship and negotiating for the crew's release, much akin to North Korea's actions when Pyongyang took the USS *Pueblo*, an American intelligence ship, in 1968. Phnom Penh could demand money or a guarantee from Washington not to attack the country or provide aid to insurgents. Pol Pot could also demonstrate that his government would not suffer any intimidation by any foreign power, including the United States.

Three of the main National Security Council members were National Security Adviser and Secretary of State Dr Henry Kissinger (right), White House Chief of Staff Donald Rumsfeld (middle), and Secretary of Defense Dr James Schlesinger (left). All helped shape final policy and decisions on the *Mayaguez*. (Ford Presidential Library)

13

Another rationale for the seizure was that a local naval commander took the initiative to board the *Mayaguez* without Phnom Penh's knowledge. The Khmer Rouge Swift boat commanders who seized the *Mayaguez* could have followed standard procedure to detain any ship within the territorial waters around Poulo Wai. Some months after the *Mayaguez* incident, Cambodian deputy premier Ieng Sary claimed the capture was a "horrible mistake" undertaken by a local commander. NSA records indicate that the first communication intercepted involving the *Mayaguez* was one from Phnom Penh to a local commander to release the crew on May 15. Sary insisted that Phnom Penh had no prior knowledge about the seizure.

"What are our options?"

Ford's May 12 morning intelligence briefing by the CIA drove the President to arrange for a meeting of the National Security Council (NSC) later that day. The NSC is the top American interagency body that discusses and decides the path of American national security policy actions. Ford met with his NSC principals: Vice President Nelson Rockefeller, Secretary of State and National Security Adviser Henry Kissinger, Secretary of Defense James Schlesinger, David Jones (the JCS chairman General George Brown was in Europe), Director Central Intelligence (DCI) William Colby, Kissinger's deputy at the NSC Lieutenant General Brent Scowcroft, White House Chief of Staff Donald Rumsfeld, and others. At the 1205hrs meeting, Ford wanted options.

NSC attendees had concerns. Kissinger's initial reaction was about getting the ship back and "how the US appears at the time." Discussion centered on ways to get Phnom Penh to release the ship through a public media demand. Most talk, however, revolved around military actions. Ford and the NSC principals debated mining Cambodian ports, using B-52s to bomb Cambodian targets, and taking a Cambodian-held island. Several attendees

The Navy commissioned the USS *Harold E. Holt*, a Knox-class frigate, in 1971. The ship was one of the first naval vessels that entered the Gulf of Thailand during the *Mayaguez* incident. The *Holt*'s small helicopter pad would prove a challenge to Air Force helicopter pilots landing marines on the ship. (US Navy)

The USS *Coral Sea*'s air wing gave Ford the ability to strike the Cambodian mainland without using Thai-based assets. Ford and Kissinger's major concerns were how fast the carrier could reach striking distance to hit the Khmer Rouge. A secondary mission was to conduct close air support missions. (US Navy)

recalled the *Pueblo* and all wanted to avoid another repeat of this incident. Kissinger seemed to downplay diplomatic action and looked for military options. The Secretary of State declared, "I am more in favor of seizing something, be it the island, the ship, or Kompong Som." The NSC meeting attendees considered some constraints. There were no aircraft carriers in the immediate area. Conducting Thai-based military operations was problematic. Bangkok was demanding that Washington remove USAF aircraft from Thailand.

Congress had also put legal restrictions on the President's ability to get America involved in war. The 1973 War Powers Resolution forced the President, within 48 hours, to report the start of military action to get congressional approval unless the United States was under imminent attack. Time was critical and Washington had little information about the Khmer Rouge's motives and strength. Ford agreed to demand publicly that Phnom Penh release both the crew and ship since he considered the Cambodian action one of piracy. At the end of the meeting, Ford looked forward to seeing detailed military options. Schlesinger would soon deliver.

Schlesinger and the JCS had already taken some actions. Aerial reconnaissance aircraft were searching for the *Mayaguez* and Thai-based USAF fighters patrolled the area. The aircraft carrier USS *Coral Sea* (CVA-43), steamed into the area, planning to arrive on May 15. This vessel could provide tactical air operations against Cambodia, its offshore position helping to avoid some of the political difficulties of US aircraft flying from Thailand. CINCPAC also directed the USS *Harold E. Holt* (DE-1074), a destroyer escort, to steam at "best speed" from its location southwest of Subic Bay, the Philippines, to the Gulf of Thailand. The USS *Hancock* (CVA-19) and accompanying ships, with a Marine Amphibious Ready Group, was assembling at Subic Bay. Unfortunately, a faulty steam valve that affected a propeller shaft limited its top speed and its role in any option was questionable. Marine units at Okinawa and Cubi Point, in the Philippines, mobilized for action. Forces were prepared while awaiting a plan. Along with USAF units in Thailand, Guam, and the Philippines, Schlesinger provided Ford with six military options.

Secretary of Defense Schlesinger's options depended on certain conditions. The primary objective was the safe return of the crew and the *Mayaguez*'s recovery. If the Khmer Rouge kept both crew and ship away from ports at

Command Relationships, May 15, 1975

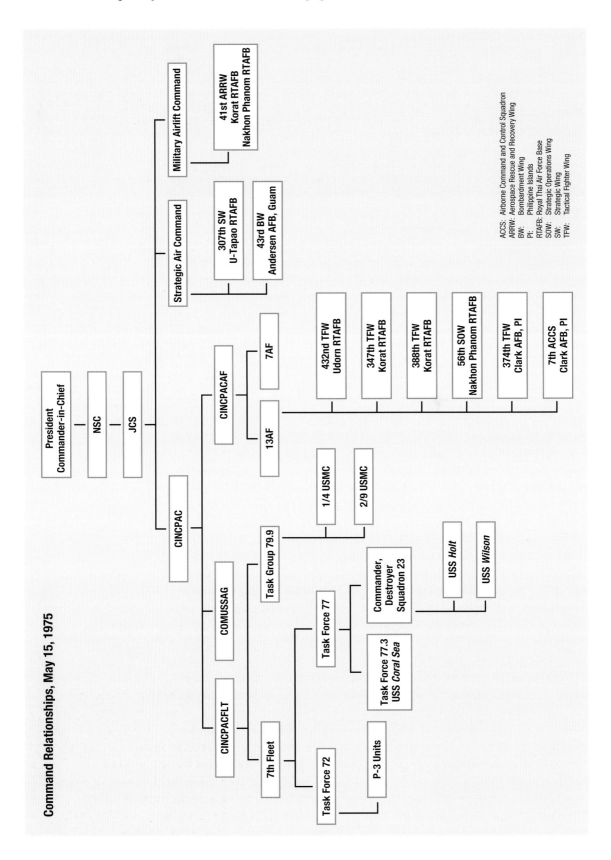

ACCS: Airborne Command and Control Squadron
ARRW: Aerospace Rescue and Recovery Wing
BW: Bombardment Wing
PI: Philippine Islands
RTAFB: Royal Thai Air Force Base
SOW: Strategic Operations Wing
SW: Strategic Wing
TFW: Tactical Fighter Wing

Kompong Som or Ream (a naval base near Kompong Som), then the US Navy could board the ship, destroy any Cambodian gunboats, and rescue the crew. Additionally, the Cambodians could also move the ship and crew to another part of the mainland or disperse the crew among several of the islands. Spreading the crew would complicate the ability to rescue them. These options were also time sensitive. Events were proceeding quickly and the President needed to make a decision.

The first option involved a direct capture of the crew and *Mayaguez* at sea. The *Holt* would confront the Cambodians and take the containerized freighter by force, if necessary. The *Holt* was within 24 hours of the area, but could receive air support from the *Coral Sea*. This course of action would display Washington's ability to protect American interests worldwide. The only force used involved the *Holt* and perhaps some carrier aviation assets. Additionally, if the action occurred offshore of Cambodia, then the legal concerns about invading sovereign territory could be minimized. This option could also result in casualties. A major fear was that Khmer Rouge forces might harm the crew if they saw the *Holt* ready to take the *Mayaguez*.

A second more ambitious option proposed involved a situation in which the Khmer Rouge sent the *Mayaguez* and crew to Kompong Som, Ream, or some other location. American military forces would include an aircraft carrier task force to impose air superiority and conduct close air support. A Marine Amphibious Brigade (MAB) consisting of 5,000 troops would seize the port. These marines from Subic Bay and Okinawa might face 1,500 to 2,000 Khmer Rouge soldiers in the area. For such a complicated assault, Defense Department officials estimated they could execute this option in five and a half days, although naval tactical air forces could begin operations within a day. Like the first option, this plan would show the nation's willingness and ability to protect American shipping and lives. The planners believed that the Khmer Rouge would probably not be able to stop this invasion. Yet this option would bring immediate public and congressional protest because of the reappearance of Americans in a conflict in Southeast Asia. Despite Department of Defense (DoD) confidence that they would prevail, American forces would suffer casualties, including the potential death

P-3 Orion aircraft, like this one, provided surveillance and tracking of targets during the incident. P-3 crews found the *Mayaguez* at Poulo Wai and followed it to Koh Tang. The P-3 could carry mines, torpedoes, and conventional bombs. Navy units flew from U-Tapao and the Philippines. (US Navy)

**MAY 12
1975**

**1418hrs
Mayaguez seized
by Khmer
Rouge forces**

of the crew and destruction of the *Mayaguez*. Attacking mainland Cambodia would also be much different than taking back an American flagged ship at sea. Ford would definitely need congressional approval for this action.

The third option was a blockade of the Cambodian coast. Air power and surface vessels could isolate Kompong Som and Ream. A naval surface task group could turn back any ships trying to enter the ports. PACFLT could implement this option immediately with the *Holt* and the USS *Vega*, a fleet replenishment ship that had also steamed into the Gulf of Thailand in response to the seizure. The Navy also had P-3 aircraft to supplement the blockade. This option was available within 24 hours. Ford could minimize potential military confrontation. Yet the option might not result in immediate release of the *Mayaguez*'s crew. In addition, the Navy might require a large force for a long time. Depending on the location of the blockading force and the extent of the blockade, some critics might consider this an act of war.

The fourth course of action advanced was the mining of Cambodian harbors. The United States had conducted aerial mining operations against North Vietnam's Haiphong harbor in December 1973 under Operation *Linebacker II*. Schlesinger noted that the *Coral Sea* and Guam based B-52Ds could drop mines or "destructors" around Kompong Som and Ream that would prevent the entry or exit by ships into both ports. Mines were stored at Subic Bay, and the *Coral Sea* would have to return to base to secure them. The USAF did have Strategic Air Command (SAC) B-52Ds at U-Tapao Air Base, in Thailand. Fear of Bangkok's opposition to using Thai-based B-52s against its neighbor limited the JCS to using Guam units, which were more than 2,000 miles away and would require additional tanker support. Ordnance crews could adjust the mines to operate for 10–180 days before they self-destructed. Pentagon planners estimated that they could start operations within 36 hours. Aircrews could emplace mines with a low probability of casualties. Mining did have some drawbacks, which ranged from the accidental sinking of neutral ships to keeping the *Mayaguez* and her crew in Kompong Som or Ream. Ford could also use a combination of blockade and mining to seal off and isolate Cambodian harbors.

Ford had a fifth option – attacking and seizing Cambodian naval and merchant ships. This "tit-for-tat" option concentrated on Khmer Rouge naval and small merchant ships operating in the Gulf of Thailand region. The *Holt*, *Vega*, and P-3 aircraft could start operations within 24 hours. Later, this force would receive more ships from the Navy's Seventh Fleet. Benefits of this option rested on its proportionality and low risk of American military casualties. However, these small ships were not the same in size or value to the *Mayaguez*, nor did the plan deter the Khmer Rouge from sinking the *Mayaguez* in revenge. Additionally, the Navy might have to tow or escort the captured ships back to American territory at Guam.

The final proposal was to seize Poulo Wai and blockade the Cambodian Hon Panjang islands. Schlesinger disclosed that a May 8 Khmer Rouge communication had indicated a desire to take Hon Panjang, and Phnom Penh also showed great interest in Poulo Wai, because of its oil. The Cambodians wanted to control the islands before the Vietnamese took them.

Assistant Secretary of Defense William Clements, in the NSC meeting, noted that Shell and Mobil oil companies had made "a significant discovery" of oil in two wells that approached 600 million to 1.5 million barrels in volume. Schlesinger offered an opinion: "The proximity of the *Mayaguez* to Poulo Wai could well have been the reason for its seizure." This option involved surrounding the islands with PACFLT assets and then securing Poulo Wai with marines. CINCPAC could use the *Holt* and *Vega* until reinforced. Marines from Subic Bay or Okinawa would then board surface ships and then make an amphibious landing or use a helicopter assault. Blockading the islands might take a day to position the *Holt*. Transit of marines might take longer, and the landing force needed additional reconnaissance. This course of action provided several advantages. Since the islands had oil, the Cambodians would be sensitive to their capture. In addition, by restricting Cambodian access to Hon Panjang, the Vietnamese had a new opportunity to make a claim to the island, which would pressure Phnom Penh to release the *Mayaguez*. Unfortunately, this option would benefit communist Vietnam.

Ford could accept a single option or could combine several options. If he did go for a military action, he would need to consult congressional leaders under the War Powers Resolution. Unfortunately, as Schlesinger would note, if the President failed to get approval by Congress or if he faced public opposition, then this situation would tarnish the ability and image of the United States worldwide. Unfortunately, the longer Ford waited, the more likely the Khmer Rouge might send the *Mayaguez* and crew to the mainland, and Washington would face protracted negotiations, as with the *Pueblo*. Without a direct communications link with the Cambodians, diplomacy might take time. Schlesinger's options did not call for Thai-based USAF capabilities. The situation, however, would all change quickly.

"This is not an easy operation"

Ford met with his NSC on May 13, twice. The Khmer Rouge had ordered Miller to move the *Mayaguez* towards Kompong Som; instead the ship ended up anchored off another island, Koh Tang. The NMCC received reports that the crew had transferred from the *Mayaguez* and it appeared the Cambodians had indeed taken them to Koh Tang. With these new reports, some of the options proposed by Schlesinger were not feasible. Other experts argued that some options would not pass Congress. Rockefeller stated, "We do not want a land war on Cambodia."

B-52Ds, based at Andersen Air Force Base in Guam, stood ready to conduct aerial mining or to drop 500lb bombs on Kompong Som or other targets in Cambodia. Some critics of the B-52D said its use was out of proportion to the incident and might raise Congressional ire. (US Air Force)

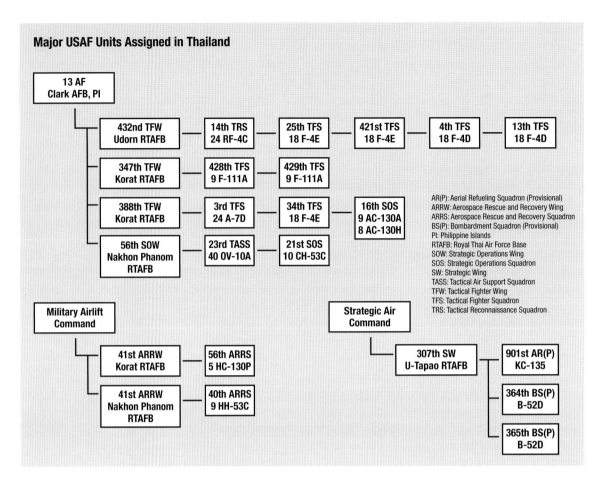

Major USAF Units Assigned in Thailand

AR(P): Aerial Refueling Squadron (Provisional)
ARRW: Aerospace Rescue and Recovery Wing
ARRS: Aerospace Rescue and Recovery Squadron
BS(P): Bombardment Squadron (Provisional)
PI: Philippine Islands
RTAFB: Royal Thai Air Force Base
SOW: Strategic Operations Wing
SOS: Strategic Operations Squadron
SW: Strategic Wing
TASS: Tactical Air Support Squadron
TFW: Tactical Fighter Wing
TFS: Tactical Fighter Squadron
TRS: Tactical Reconnaissance Squadron

There was concern about taking too long to act. Rockefeller commented, "The longer we take, the worse it gets." There was no definite proof that the *Mayaguez* crew was still on the ship, imprisoned on Koh Tang, headed to Kompong Som, or that the Cambodians had split up the crew. Ford decided on several immediate actions. First, aircraft would stop any vessels from leaving Koh Tang. This would require using Thai-based USAF units, since the *Coral Sea*'s aircraft were not in range. Second, the President ordered the military to stop all ship traffic moving to and around Koh Tang. Third, Ford told the NSC to prepare to land on the *Mayaguez* the next morning. Fourth, he ordered the JCS to get ready to take Koh Tang. Some marines had already landed via C-141 aircraft at U-Tapao; others would follow. The only means to land on the ship was by USAF helicopters from rescue and special operations units. Kissinger told Ford that the Thai government was demanding an explanation about the marines on U-Tapao. Ford wanted to land the marines at night to take back the ship. Jones' reaction to all of these actions was that "This is not an easy operation."

By May 13, diplomatic efforts seemed to have failed. A day earlier, Kissinger had sent a demand for the release of the crew and ship through the PRC's liaison office in Washington to Phnom Penh. The Chinese chief of the liaison office refused to accept the letter. George H. W. Bush, chief of the

Koh Tang is a small island that had few distinguishing landmarks. The island had limited natural landing zones and a thick jungle canopy hindered close air support efforts. This view of the island is from the *Holt*. Gunfire support is visible on the West Beach area. (US Navy)

US liaison office in China, tried to deliver the same message to the Chinese government and the Cambodian embassy in Beijing. Both attempts failed. The United States also tried to get United Nations Secretary General Kurt Waldheim to intervene, but that would take time. Waldheim cautioned the United States not to take immediate action. The Cambodians did not respond. Diplomacy appeared dead.

Later that evening, Ford met again with the NSC. The situation had changed yet again. USAF aircraft tried to stop a fishing boat with 30–40 passengers, which appeared to have "Caucasians" on board, headed for Kompong Som. The aircraft sank escorting gunboats, but they failed to stop the fishing vessel – rather than attempt to disable it and possibly kill Americans, the pilots allowed it to pass. Ford was upset that the ship had escaped Koh Tang, despite his previous order. Kissinger recommended all ships around Koh Tang sunk. Despite a question by White House aide John Marsh that Americans may be on board some of those ships, Kissinger responded, "I think the pilot should sink them. He should destroy the boats and not send situation reports."

The Secretary of State pushed for invading Koh Tang and Kompong Som. Jones had already started planning the details on the options given to Ford. The situation was complicated because the *Hancock* was having mechanical problems and could not reach Koh Tang in time. Schlesinger thought that using B-52s would raise "red flags" in Congress and collateral damage might be too severe. Discussion also centered on bombing Kompong Som and Ream airfields both to ensure that no support was available to Khmer Rouge on Koh Tang and to punish the Cambodians. Ford would soon approve this option; the question was whether to use *Coral Sea* naval aviators or B-52s from Guam. Ford authorized the military mission to proceed the next day.

Intelligence: The key to planning

Uncertainty clouded the decision-making abilities of Ford and his advisers regarding military actions. American intelligence about the Cambodian intentions, military strength and disposition, and *Mayaguez* crew location was partial. USAF and Navy reconnaissance and patrol aircraft had located the ship, but they could not determine where the Khmer Rouge had taken the crew. Patrolling AC-130s used infrared imaging devices which indicated that there was no heat coming from the *Mayaguez*'s smokestacks. As the ship had no power, the crew was therefore probably not on board. The NSC could not dismiss the possibility of crew members on Koh Tang, despite reports of the fishing boat approaching Kompong Som.

MAY 13
1975

1640–1700hrs
Crew removed
from the
Mayaguez

AMERICAN STRIKING POWER IN THE GULF OF THAILAND

Washington had to overcome significant distances to conduct the *Mayaguez* operation, and hence relied heavily on American airpower. Helicopters, for example, provided the means to transport marines to Koh Tang and the *Holt*. Another asset was the USAF and Navy attack, bomber, fighter, and reconnaissance aircraft that allowed Washington to find and hit targets throughout the region. The USAF's 7AF controlled scores of aircraft in Southeast Asia throughout its command area during the Vietnam War. By 1975, however, it was a shadow of its former self, and relocated to Thailand, although during the *Mayaguez* incident it was augmented by taking operational control of 13AF aircraft.

Two of the major USAF workhorses were the A-7D and F-4. The A-7D could deliver 15,000lb of external ordnance at a range of 1,430 miles. Its 1,000-round 20mm M61A1 Vulcan cannon and payload offered a superb ability to conduct close air support and interdiction. Like the A-7D, the F-4 Phantom II multirole aircraft had a naval background, and could carry up to 16,000lb of external stores, including four supersonic air-to-air missiles. The F-4E mounted its 20mm cannon internally, while its older brother, the F-4D, used an external gun pod. The RF-4C reconnaissance version used medium- to long-range oblique angle cameras. CINCPAC called on F-4D, F-4E, and RF-4Cs to conduct air superiority, close air support, interdiction, and photographic reconnaissance missions. Due to their intensive use, the F-4 and RF-4 had the highest loss rates in Vietnam, accounting for more than 20 percent of fixed-wing losses.

Two other USAF aircraft that gave 7AF an advantage were the F-111A and AC-130. The F-111A had a troubled history. Conceived as a multirole, multiservice aircraft, it had severe developmental problems, and the Navy eventually cancelled its participation. The F-111A's initial 1968 Vietnam deployment, under Operation *Combat Lancer*, resulted in three aircraft losses. One of the aircraft was lost on its first combat mission. Once engineers solved its technical issues, the F-111A became an outstanding all weather, low-level strike aircraft capable of carrying 30,000lb of weapons. The F-111A Aardvark returned to conduct very effective missions against Hanoi during the 1972 *Linebacker* bombing campaign.

Calls for better night-time close air support led to conversion of C-119 and C-47 transports to gunships during the Vietnam War. The AC-130 Spectre was an extension of this development. The AC-130A had two 20mm and two 40mm cannon, as wel as a pair of miniguns with tracking and radar systems. The AC-130H also had an M102 105mm howitzer with 100 rounds. The aircraft could loiter over a target for about two hours with a 45-minute fuel reserve. Thai-based AC-130s attacked the Ho Chi Minh trail at night.

The Navy also flew variants of the F-4 and A-7, and operated the Grumman A-6A Intruder that replaced the venerable A-1 Skyraider. The A-6A bomber used its Digital Integrated Attack Navigation Equipment to deliver its 17,000lb payload at night and under bad weather. Intruders flew low-level against targets throughout North Vietnam.

Landing, occupying, and searching Koh Tang required a rapid assault. The number of marines needed for the assault depended on the size, disposition, and armament of any Khmer Rouge defenders. Initial reports concerning the strength of the defenders varied. One report, actually used by the marines who eventually landed on Koh Tang, indicated only 18–30 irregular forces. This information, based on an account from a former Lon Nol naval officer, was out of date. The Commander, Intelligence Pacific (IPAC) indicated that there might be 90–100 Khmer Rouge with unknown numbers of 82mm mortars, 75mm recoilless rifles, rocket-propelled grenades (RPGs), and machine guns. The DIA estimated a higher number of enemy forces, at 150–200, with similar heavy armaments to those mentioned in IPAC's report. Additionally, an orbiting AC-130 gunship, using its sensors, reported a sizeable ground force on Koh Tang during the early evening on

May 13. The Air Force crew estimated that the Cambodians had three gun emplacements positioned in a 100yd curve.

Cambodian forces also had gunboats and some aircraft. An end-of-tour report by Brigadier General William Palmer, dated April 30, 1975, indicated that the Cambodians had 22 T-28 propeller-driven aircraft and six AC-47 gunships. These aircraft could potentially attack marines on Koh Tang, but their operational status was questionable due to a lack of pilots and poor maintenance. The NSC was nevertheless concerned about these aircraft, and used them as a justification to attack Kompong Som and Ream.

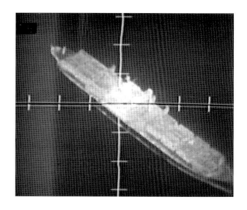

America: Limited forces, limited options

CINCPAC would plan, coordinate, and control the major elements of any operation. PACFLT had few ships in the area. Major combatants included the *Holt* and the guided-missile destroyer *Henry B. Wilson* (DDG-7), ordered to head to the area on May 13, and the *Coral Sea* and her escorts which were steaming to the Gulf of Thailand. *Coral Sea* aircraft included 10 A-6A bombers in VA-95, 24 A-7Es in VA-22 and VA-94, and F-4Ns in VF-51 and VF-111. The *Hancock* and the amphibious assault ship *Okinawa* (LPH-3) were not available due to mechanical problems. PACFLT also controlled VP-4's P-3 aircraft, which operated in the area.

USMC forces were available to support the military options. From Cubi Point in the Philippines, a reinforced company of five officers and 115 enlisted marines from the 1st Battalion, 4th Marines (1/4 Marines) had departed to Thailand. The 2/9 Marines would later arrive at U-Tapao from Okinawa. This force was sufficient to take the *Mayaguez* and land troops on Koh Tang.

The largest contingent available for operations was from the USAF. The 13th Air Force (13AF) at Clark Air Base in the Philippines controlled tactical and special operations units in Thailand. Thai-based units included the 432nd Tactical Fighter Wing (TFW) at Udorn; the 347th TFW, 388th TFW, and 56th Aerospace Rescue and Recovery Squadron (ARRS) at Korat; and the 56th Special Operations Wing (SOW) and the 40th ARRS at Nakhon Phanom. SAC maintained the 307th Strategic Wing (SW) with KC-135 tankers and B-52Ds at U-Tapao. They were not under CINCPAC's control. Similarly, SAC's 43rd SW at Andersen Air Force Base in Guam was available to conduct B-52D bombing missions and KC-135 tanker support. Clark also supplied EC-130 airborne command and control aircraft to manage all combat operations. Likewise, the USAF's Military Airlift Command provided transportation by C-141 to the marines to move them from Okinawa and the Philippines to U-Tapao. National assets also included U-2 reconnaissance aircraft.

Thai-based AC-130s used their low-light level television sensors to observe the *Mayaguez*. These sensors helped target ships or soldiers at night, and enabled the AC-130 to attack with great accuracy with weapons ranging from howitzers to miniguns. The AC-130 would prove invaluable throughout the operation. (US Air Force)

THE PLAN

Ford, the NSC, CINCPAC staffers, and commanders in Thailand and at sea began to develop detailed operational concepts, which evolved into plans to send America into combat in Southeast Asia once again. Despite evolving conditions around the Sea of Thailand, the CINCPAC staff developed a plan to meet Ford's objectives. Coordination between Washington, CINCPAC, Thailand, and forces afloat demanded precise timing. Retaking the *Mayaguez*, assaulting Koh Tang, searching for and rescuing the crew, and

Air Force Security Police, from Nakhon Phanom, volunteered to retake the *Mayaguez*. While trying to move forces to U-Tapao, a CH-53C transporting these volunteers crashed when the main rotor separated. All onboard died. The marines would have to board the ship and try to rescue the crew. (US Air Force)

bombing targets on Kompong Som and Ream would require precision command and control.

While the staffs exchanged ideas, external events shaped the final operational concept. The need to attempt a rescue without the *Okinawa* or the *Hancock* limited CINCPAC options – Thai-based USAF aircraft had to replace these Navy assets. Air Force rescue and special operations helicopters would instead move marines from U-Tapao to Koh Tang, where they would take the *Mayaguez*. Tactical aircraft from Thailand were designated to provide close air support and interdiction. JCS directives had already pushed CINCPAC to conduct reconnaissance missions, and USAF A-7D, F-4D/E, and F-111A aircraft had strafed and bombed Cambodian ships to isolate Koh Tang. Special operations AC-130A/Hs and F-111As watched Cambodian movements at night – Washington had already moved beyond considering Thai sensitivities.

The 7AF under Lieutenant General John Burns would control all Thai-based USAF units. Burns was also head of the United States Support Activities Group (USSAG). USAAG had inherited the role of the Military Assistance Command, Vietnam (MACV). Gayler designated Burns as the overall mission commander in charge of the assault on Koh Tang and boarding the *Mayaguez*. Burns had begun planning a rescue attempt even before Ford examined the options. USAF helicopters at Nakhon Phanom moved to U-Tapao to support the operation. Airmen from the 656th Security Police Squadron at Nakhon Phanom had volunteered to board the *Mayaguez* as an alternative plan. Tragically, on May 13 at 2130hrs, a CH-53C crashed 36 miles east of the base, killing all aboard including 18 of the volunteer Air Force security policemen for the mission and five helicopter crew members. The loss of life and a valuable helicopter would obviously affect the final plan, limiting the means to carry marines and reinforce them.

The distance from U-Tapao to Koh Tang is 190 nautical miles. A HH-53C or CH-53C would require about one hour and forty minutes to cross the distance. This meant a round trip of about four hours to resupply or reinforce any marine units on the island. Any further helicopter losses through combat or mechanical issues would severely disrupt operations.

Operational concept

The JCS-defined mission to CINCPAC was simply to retake the *Mayaguez*. Jones also directed CINCPAC to conduct military operations "to influence the outcome of US initiatives to secure the release of the ship's crew." Given this mission statement, CINCPAC had wide latitude to plan and change operations. The JCS provided Ford with an initial operational concept, but more detailed planning was needed.

Jones had notified CINCPAC to start all military operations on May 15 at sunrise. The marines were front and center in recapturing the *Mayaguez* and invading Koh Tang. The original plan to retake the ship

This topside view of the *Mayaguez* shows the difficulty of trying to land helicopters directly on her. The aluminum containers could not support a helicopter's weight. The bow and aft were too small. Having marines use ropes to land was too risky. Boarding by the *Holt* was the only viable option. (US Navy)

envisioned using six USAF helicopters, but the Nakhon Phanom loss and some maintenance problems reduced the force to three. One option was to place the helicopters directly on the *Mayaguez*. The only area for a helicopter to land was on the containers, but unfortunately the helicopter's weight on an aluminum cargo container might cause it to collapse. An alternative was to have the marines use ropes to deploy onto the freighter while the helicopters hovered. If Khmer Rouge forces were on the ship, however, then they could easily shoot at the helicopters and anyone leaving them.

Helicopter deployment was rejected. Instead, the marine force from the Philippines, Company D of the 1/4 Marines, under Captain Walter J. Wood, would therefore arrive on and board the *Mayaguez* from the *Holt*. This plan involved using 48 marines, 12 Navy and Military Sealift Command (MSC) personnel, a USAF explosive ordnance disposal (EOD)

THE KHMER ROUGE

The Khmer Rouge (meaning "Red Khmer," the Khmer being a major ethnic group in Cambodia) started as a fringe communist group in rural areas in Cambodia. Their rise to power came about due to the actions of Cambodian generals under Lon Nol, who overthrew Prince Norodom Sihanouk. Sihanouk supported the Khmer Rouge in his quest to return to power. The Khmer Rouge, formed by Pol Pot, would eventually kill between one and two million people – no one truly knows how many Cambodians and foreigners lost their lives under the Khmer Rouge. Their goal was to return Cambodia, later renamed the Democratic Republic of Kampuchea, to the more simple life of an agrarian state. Pol Pot also wanted to eliminate all Western influences.

The Khmer Rouge, aided by the North Vietnamese and VC, started a communist insurgency against the Lon Nol government in 1970. This insurgency successfully controlled about one third of the country. For five years, Lon Nol, supported by Washington, battled the Khmer Rouge and Vietnamese. American secret bombings in 1973, the ceasefire with the United States, the growing number and success of Khmer Rouge insurgents, and the desire to capture South Vietnam caused Hanoi to move away from Cambodia. The Khmer Rouge took up the slack and they continued their war against Lon Nol. Pol Pot's Khmer Rouge eventually forced Lon Nol from power and Phnom Penh fell in April 1975. Many of the Khmer Rouge followers were teenagers and children. The implementation of Pol Pot's deadly policies took on an even more sinister face when these young communists administered them.

Under the Khmer Rouge, any Cambodian government workers, business owners, educators, or those who disagreed with the regime were marked for arrest, torture, and death. The Khmer Rouge also wanted to kill any intellectuals. Suspicion fell on any Cambodian who spoke a foreign language, since that ability indicated an education. Religion was banned, especially Buddhism. No one could own personal property. Cambodians wearing glasses, using a watch, or possessing any other technology also met with instant death.

After taking control of the country, the communists eventually abandoned cities and closed any facilities that used modern technology. The country was reborn from "Year Zero." Schools, monasteries, temples, and businesses closed. The Khmer Rouge rebuilt society by sending citizens to rural agricultural camps and farms. Mass evacuations moved the population to these ideologically run collective farms and a brutal life without money and material goods. Phnom Penh's aim was to triple food production to become self-reliant. One of the only countries that maintained a very limited, distant relationship with Phnom Penh was China. In reality, the collective farms became death camps. Any sign of disobedience would end a worker's life. Many died due to overwork, starvation, and disease. The reign of terror ended in 1979. Continued border skirmishes with the Vietnamese and crimes against humanity forced the Vietnamese to intervene. Pol Pot faced arrest and trial, but he only served house arrest, and died in April 1998.

team, and an Army Cambodian linguist. The Navy and MSC crew would operate the recaptured ship and help move it out of the area. Planners feared that the Khmer Rouge might have placed explosives on board the vessel, and they would detonate these if the Americans attempted to take it. The EOD team, therefore, would search the vessel and make it safe if need be. Photographs from reconnaissance aircraft helped identify 30 Cambodians on board. The *Holt* and her crew could support the marines if they were in a fight. Once the *Mayaguez* was under American control, the *Holt* would then escort it to safety.

The main effort of the operation was a marine assault on Koh Tang. Helicopter availability reduced the assault force to eight CH-53C and HH-53C aircraft. Along with the accident loss and maintenance problems, the USAF had to keep some helicopters in reserve for rescue and recovery operations. The first assault wave would set 175 marines on the island. Other waves would deliver additional marines, ultimately deploying a total force of 625 marines and 25 other personnel. The initial wave would secure opposite sides of the island and search an area that included a fishing village where the Khmer Rouge might hold the *Mayaguez* crew.

These operations required support from the USAF and the Navy. 7AF assets could provide day and night aircraft coverage over Koh Tang and the *Mayaguez*. Their main mission was to give close air support to the marine ground support force on the island. USAF aircraft would prevent movement by any small Cambodian watercraft in the Koh Tang and Poulo Wai area. Planners also assigned Thai-based HC-130P and at least two HH-53C aircraft for search-and-rescue operations. Naval vessels would provide offshore gunfire support.

SAC units in Thailand and Guam also had support missions. The approved JCS concept included four B-52D cells of three aircraft to attack Kompong Som harbor, Phumi Phsar Ream naval base, and Ream airfield. Later plans specified one cell each against Ream airfield and naval base. SAC planners readied the other six aircraft for Kompong Som. Twelve KC-135 tankers supported the attack force. The initial B-52 attack would occur three hours after the first assault on Koh Tang. SAC tankers from Thailand would also refuel any 7AF jets. The plan called for continuous coverage by at least one EC-130 to serve as an on-scene mission coordinator. The final operational concept also included authorization to use the BLU-82, a 15,000lb conventional bomb designed to clear a landing zone for helicopters from dense jungle terrain. Philippines-based C-130 aircraft would deploy the weapon from a parachute.

US Navy carrier aviation also played a major role in the operation. Like the 7AF aircraft, carrier A-6A and A-7E aircraft from the *Coral Sea* had authorization to restrict Cambodian shipping movements around the Koh Tang and Poulo Wai islands. Naval aviation, when in range, would also conduct daytime armed reconnaissance missions in the area. Ford might have the option to use *Coral Sea* aircraft strikes on Kompong Som and the Ream complexes. He had to choose between B-52D and *Coral Sea* aircraft to attack the Cambodian coast.

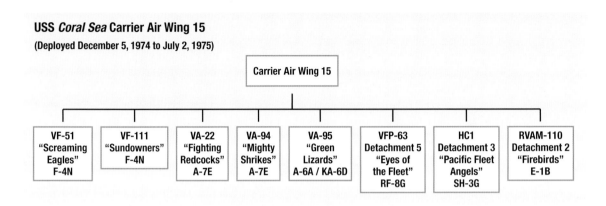

USS *Coral Sea* Carrier Air Wing 15
(Deployed December 5, 1974 to July 2, 1975)

			Carrier Air Wing 15				

| VF-51 "Screaming Eagles" F-4N | VF-111 "Sundowners" F-4N | VA-22 "Fighting Redcocks" A-7E | VA-94 "Mighty Shrikes" A-7E | VA-95 "Green Lizards" A-6A / KA-6D | VFP-63 Detachment 5 "Eyes of the Fleet" RF-8G | HC1 Detachment 3 "Pacific Fleet Angels" SH-3G | RVAM-110 Detachment 2 "Firebirds" E-1B |

The final and crucial determination centered on the command and control structure. Ford gave CINCPAC overall control of the operation, and the JCS also designated Commander USSAG (COMUSSAG)/7AF as the on-scene coordinating authority for all supporting forces. CINCPAC staff on Hawaii had to control activities regarding CINCPAC, COMUSSAG/7AF, and the marine forces operating in Thailand and on Koh Tang. The only major command and control element outside of CINCPAC was the SAC B-52D force at Guam.

Conflicting priorities

The mission concept was not without controversy. Local commanders using the concept to make detailed plans would need more information and required extensive coordination. Some of their concerns led to options that delayed decisions or forced commanders to adapt rapidly to changing requirements or events. Still, the priority of the mission rested on safely rescuing all of the crew.

Another priority included avoiding casualties, friendly and civilian. One of the lingering psychological remnants of the Vietnam War was the American public's aversion to casualties. Ford and Kissinger, however, were

A-7Ds, like these, gave CINCPAC a variety of capabilities to strike the Khmer Rouge. The A-7Ds from the 388th TFW provided close air support and interdicted boats in the area. A month after the incident, the Thai government forced America to start pulling aircraft out of the country. (US Air Force)

also advocating the bombing of the Cambodian mainland, partly to restrict Khmer Rouge reinforcement or thwart any air or naval threat, despite overwhelming American air superiority and growing naval strength in the area. The final priority was American/Thai relations. Bangkok had allowed American military forces to maintain a foothold in Southeast Asia, despite Washington's retreat from Cambodia and Vietnam. Maintaining good relations with any country, especially ones bordering communist states, would potentially be difficult after the *Mayaguez* rescue.

Washington had several operational objectives and priorities that came into direct conflict with one another. Accidental bombing of a ship or an inadvertent firefight on Koh Tang might kill members of the *Mayaguez*'s crew; bombing Kompong Som and Ream could achieve the same result. Similarly, Khmer Rouge defenders could exact revenge on the crew members or the ship once military operations began. A direct assault on Koh Tang and the ship might result in an unacceptable number of Americans killed or wounded – the CH-53C helicopter crash had already cost 23 Americans lives even before any rescue attempt. The initial wave of marines landing on Koh Tang faced an indeterminate number of Cambodian defenders. In addition, using B-52Ds to bomb an urban area could inflict heavy civilian casualties, harden Cambodian resistance, and turn world and domestic opinion against Washington. Keeping the Bangkok government placated was also at odds with the need to use USAF-based assets at U-Tapao and staging marines from Thailand to take the ship and lead the assault on the island.

Time and uncertainty weighed heavily on Washington. Dynamic events dictated changes to the priorities. For such a complex set of interrelated

When the F-111A first deployed to Southeast Asia, it was plagued by problems with its terrain-following radar, causing several aircraft to crash. By 1975, the Air Force fixed the problem and they served admirably. The F-111s would provide close air support and interdict boats. (US Air Force)

MAY 14 1975

c.1645hrs President Ford orders operation to commence

activities, there was no written operational plan provided to or discussed by the CINCPAC and other forces that would ultimately conduct the rescue of the *Mayaguez* and her crew. The JCS, CINCPAC, COMUSSAG/7AF, PACFLT, and the marines needed more than concept, they required a detailed plans and actions.

Taking Koh Tang

Koh Tang is about 3.5 miles long and 2 miles wide. It sits approximately 27 nautical miles from the Cambodian coast. Jungle-covered terrain dominated the island, with a small rise in the center, designated Hill 440. Before the Khmer Rouge had taken control of Cambodia, the island had a small communications site and was home to limited fishing activity. The northern area also contained two relatively shallow beaches on the east and west coasts. The East Beach had a longer, coral sand beach that could serve as a main landing zone. The West Beach was much smaller, but if the marines could land simultaneously on both beaches, then they could drive towards the center, take the fishing village, and possibly rescue any *Mayaguez* crew members. The East Beach cove area had also been the location where the Khmer Rouge had removed the *Mayaguez* crew by fishing boat. The marines noticed that the East and West Beaches were the best approaches to take Koh Tang; so did the Khmer Rouge.

Men from 2/9 Marines in Okinawa began to get ready for deployment on the afternoon of May 13. At U-Tapao, Colonel John M. Johnson, the designated USMC ground force commander, had ordered Lieutenant Colonel Randall W. Austin, the 2nd Battalion commander, to get his force to Thailand. Ten C-141s moved Austin's battalion and other elements from Kadena Air Base to U-Tapao throughout May 14. Six other C-141s also transported 118.3 short tons of equipment, supplies, and ammunition from Okinawa to Thailand to support the operation. Austin's force totaled 1,095 personnel. The force was designated Battalion Landing Team (BLT) 2/9. BLT 2/9 included troops that had just completed field-training exercises in Okinawa. The marine force included E and G Companies, headquarters elements, a heavy weapons section to include 4.2in and 81mm mortars, and other support teams.

Austin's mission was to take Koh Tang and hold it for at least 48 hours. His marines would then search the island for any captives. They would also ensure that Khmer Rouge forces did not interfere with the *Mayaguez* boarding action by firing upon the ship from the island – the attack on Koh Tang would occur simultaneously with the boarding of the *Mayaguez*. The 40th ARRS and 21st Special Operations Squadron (SOS) only had 11 operating helicopters. With three helicopters assigned to 1/4's transport to the *Holt*, Austin therefore had only eight helicopters to conduct the first of three planned assault waves. The first wave would send Company G onto the East and West Beaches; the planned attack force included 163 marines, 11 Navy corpsmen, and three Army translators. Captain James H. Davis, the Company G commander, and a reinforced platoon would land with two helicopters on the West Beach. The rest of Company G would land on the east end with the rest of the helicopters. A second wave would bring in Company E. The third wave would end the assault, which in total would put about 625 marines and 25 other personnel on the island.

Completing a helicopter assault against an unknown enemy force, one that may have had time to entrench itself, was an uncertain challenge. To avoid accidently killing captive *Mayaguez* crew members and to achieve surprise, the first assault wave would dispense with any naval gunfire support or pre-invasion air attacks to soften up Cambodian defenses. Once on the island, a Marine forward air controller (FAC) could direct USAF close air support and any naval gunfire support from the *Holt* and the *Wilson*. Later, the *Coral Sea* attack squadrons could provide additional firepower. The onsite FAC would have good situational awareness and local information to direct accurate fire. In an attempt to enhance mission intelligence, Austin had conducted an afternoon aerial reconnaissance over Koh Tang on May 14. Using a handheld 35mm camera, he flew over the densely forested area at 6,000ft in an Army U-21 airplane. This minimum altitude was above effective enemy antiaircraft fire, but it was also too high to photograph any details on the island. The island had no discernable landmarks; the jungle foliage had created an effective defensive cover for the Khmer Rouge.

If the initial intelligence estimate of about 18–30 Khmer Rouge defenders on Koh Tang were true, then the marines' attack would have no problem overwhelming them. There is some question about whether anyone provided the IPAC or DIA estimates to Johnson and Austin. A 307th SW intelligence officer had briefed the Air Force helicopter crews and allegedly, a marine officer was present. Unfortunately, the island landing planners did not have this vital piece of information about Cambodian ground strength, details that may have changed Austin's plan. The marines did not envision landing on a defended beach area emplaced with heavy weapons. Reinforcements, if required, might take more than two hours to arrive due to the helicopter transit time.

Khmer Rouge forces had actually built several defensive positions on Koh Tang; Cambodian military units had to defend the territory against potential Vietnamese incursions. On the island, the Khmer Rouge battalion commander, Em Son, nominally had 450 soldiers. The battalion was part of the Khmer Rouge's 3rd Division, assigned to the Cambodian coastal areas. During the *Mayaguez* incident, however, he had no more than 100 defenders. Em Son's men had a variety of weapons, which included captured American military stocks. The garrison had created a trench system along the East and West Beaches, dotted with three-man fighting positions and bunkers. The defensive lines also included overlapping fields of fire from entrenched machine-gun positions and mortars. Ammunition storage areas supported the trench defenses. The Khmer Rouge headquarters was near Hill 440 along with a radio site.

The planned execution time for the rescue mission, calculated by the JCS, was 0542hrs on May 15. This time was the four minutes before Koh Tang official sunrise. Unfortunately, the dawn breaks about 20–30 minutes before this time, so there was the danger that the Khmer Rouge defenders might be able to see the first wave's helicopters arriving and take immediate action. The first wave of helicopters would leave U-Tapao at 0414hrs that day. Plans called for the last wave of the initial marine assault force to depart at 0423hrs. The marines would deploy in three helicopter flights. The first three HH-53Cs would go to the *Holt* and carry out the *Mayaguez* recapture team. Five HH-53C and CH-53Cs would land the initial marine force on Koh Tang. The simultaneous boarding of the *Mayaguez* would require additional time. Some of the USAF helicopter crews had experience landing their aircraft on the aircraft carrier *Midway* during Operation *Frequent Wind*, the evacuation from South Vietnam. The *Midway*'s landing deck, however, was much larger than the small helicopter pad on the *Holt*. Transferring Company D might be difficult, especially in the early daylight. The *Holt* also had to close on the *Mayaguez* and allow Wood's men to gain access to the ship.

Once BLT 2/9's mission was complete, the JCS would extract the marines. The NSC was still apprehensive about alienating Bangkok by using U-Tapao as a base of military operations against Cambodia. There was no hiding from Bangkok the use of 7AF and SAC resources from Thailand in the operation, since Thai forces also used the airfields. The Thai government had already asked questions about Company D's arrival at U-Tapao. Austin's battalion created more angst among the Thais. JCS planners advanced two options: marine recovery on the *Coral Sea* or return to Thailand. Sending the marines to the *Coral Sea* would avoid angering the Thais again. As the aircraft carrier moved closer to Koh Tang, the extraction might not require as much time as the return to Thailand and the carrier could provide more support. In addition, Navy maintenance crews could help repair and refuel any helicopters. Medical support was also available to any wounded personnel. The return to Thailand therefore became a last resort.

Attacking the mainland

The other major elements of the operation were to be a series of attacks on several locations on the Cambodian coast, including Kompong Som and the Ream area complexes. CIA analysts had discounted Kompong Som as an active port. Its main activity was a resupply point for the VC and Khmer Rouge naval ships. The original reason to attack the harbor and airfields was to restrict any possible Cambodian reinforcement or interference with American military actions around Koh Tang. American bombing could also convince Phnom Penh to release the crew, or else the Cambodian capital might be the next target. A more strategic reason was a demonstration of American resolve – bombing Cambodia was a message to Phnom Penh and others that Washington had the political will and military means to retaliate globally. Kissinger and other NSC members had discussed the impact of the *Mayaguez* incident in relation to North Korea. With America's seeming defeat in Southeast Asia, Washington wanted to demonstrate to Pyongyang not to confuse the Vietnam withdrawal with an unwillingness to defend South Korea.

The attack on the Ream airfield was of questionable value. The only Cambodian aircraft that might attack were T-28s, AC-47s, and some possible helicopter gunships. These aircraft had limited armament, serviceability, and operational capability, and the 7AF and *Coral Sea* F-4 combat air patrols over the Gulf of Thailand would make short work of them. Furthermore, both the *Holt* and *Wilson* had surface-to-air missiles that covered the area around Koh Tang and the *Mayaguez*. Jones and DCI Colby both argued that the Cambodian aircraft at Ream did not seem to be a major threat and opposed an attack on the airfield. White House Chief of Staff Donald Rumsfeld, however, pressed the point that if the Cambodians had the capability to launch military aircraft from the airport, then Washington had a "stronger argument" to bomb it. The Ream airfield remained a target.

The only unanswered question was the use of B-52s or the *Coral Sea* aircraft. The long distance from Guam, potential collateral damage and conflict escalation, and the prospect of congressional opposition convinced Ford to drop the B-52 option. B-52s carried more bombs than naval aircraft, but their value was in hitting area targets. A B-52 cell of three planes typically carried about 108 500lb bombs apiece. Jones had mentioned at an NSC meeting that the only targets of value seemed to be at the harbor of Kompong Som. RF-4C photo-reconnaissance jets had overflown the area, and spotted two freighters in port. Although the B-52 might not target the ships, there was a chance of them being hit by errant bombs. This unintended damage might affect the public perception of America's military action, especially if the ships were vessels for neutral countries. Ford still wanted to use the B-52s, but settled on the naval carrier aircraft to conduct the mission. CINCSAC keep the Guam-based B-52s on a one-hour alert.

The *Coral Sea* had a stock of precision guided munitions (PGMs), such as the AGM-62 Walleye television-guided bomb and Paveway laser-guided bombs. PGMs offered Ford the ability to destroy specific buildings, warehouses, and other storage facilities. Chief of Naval Operations Admiral James L. Holloway had reported to Ford that the *Coral Sea* had 81 PGMs onboard, plenty to sustain several missions. The Navy pilots would reduce any collateral damage in the mission by deploying these weapons. Using carrier aircraft also allowed CINCPAC to cycle the *Coral Sea* A-6A and A-7Es to step up bombing missions.

Jones' plan would send *Coral Sea* aircraft into the Kompong Som area and Ream around the time of the *Mayaguez* boarding. The NSC directed the JCS to have the *Coral Sea* aircraft's time on target as 0745hrs for the first mission. Jones designated the first mission as "armed reconnaissance" and subsequent missions to include strikes against multiple targets. The targets included enemy aircraft at the Ream airfield, port areas, railway facilities, warehouses, and other buildings. Since no one could positively identify the two ships at Kompong Som harbor, they were left alone. Subsequent witnesses identified the ships as Chinese.

A RF-4C photographed the area where the Khmer Rouge might hold the *Mayaguez*'s crew, in an abandoned fishing village. This would be the marines' center of attention for the helicopter assault. The Khmer Rouge did not hold any captives on Koh Tang. Notice the RF-4C shadow in the right bottom. (US Air Force)

At a May 14 NSC meeting, the CIA estimated that approximately 2,000 Khmer Rouge forces defended the Kompong Som area with a potential for adding another 14,000 soldiers from southwest Cambodia. Air defenses around Kompong Som and Ream were minimal. The Cambodians possessed 23mm and 37mm antiaircraft guns, and CIA analysts identified a single 37mm gun south of Kompong Som and two 37mm gun sites at Ream airfield. The effective range for these weapons was 3 nautical miles, capable of hitting targets under 14,000ft. Navy aircrew would not face any surface-to-air missiles. A-6A and A-7E crews could launch PGMs at enough distance from the targets to avoid any antiaircraft artillery rounds. The Khmer Rouge also had no interceptors capable of shooting down jets, so the air threat seemed negligible. Cambodian naval forces in port at Kompong Som and Ream, on the eve of the attack, were limited to 13 coastal patrol boats, ten riverine patrol boats, and one submarine chaser. These vessels did not appear to offer much opposition to any American attack. However, the Khmer Rouge could call on several landing craft, which could move about 2,400 soldiers and reach Koh Tang in four hours.

Discussion among NSC members on May 14 had included using the *Coral Sea* aircraft to attack Phnom Penh. The President quickly dismissed this option, since he wanted to focus on protecting the operation from any Cambodian reinforcements deploying from Kompong Som. In addition, if the Navy pilots struck only military targets, then there was little chance of killing any *Mayaguez* crew members, based on the strong assumption that they were not held in military facilities. Kissinger had, before the May 14 NSC meeting, a conversation with Ford in which he pressed the President to conduct the air strikes on Kompong Som. Ultimately, Ford would agree with Kissinger. At an 1145hrs meeting in the Oval Office, Kissinger thought the JCS would not pursue the attacks. He thought they suffered from the "McNamara syndrome," and that they would "not be so ferocious." Dr Kissinger also called Gayler "disastrous," showing little confidence in the CINCPAC leadership to conduct the operation – the secretary wanted action.

Command, control, and communications

By 1975, technical advances in communications had allowed Washington to talk to a regional commander or individual platoon commander in the field. The *Mayaguez* incident had national security implications that caught Ford's attention. The operation's command and control systems were complicated, as the operation was one of the first in which the highest levels of government could oversee tactical decisions. The implications were enormous. Senior officers could direct or countermand orders from subordinate commanders to their units. Demands for information might swamp communications systems. Similarly, decision-makers had access to both unfiltered and properly analyzed information.

The command and control system relied on a number of secure voice, teletype, and satellite communications systems. The White House had governance over all forces through the NMCC – the Pentagon control center issued orders from the President to CINCPAC. Coincidentally, Gayler was in

The HH-53C played a major role during the assault and extraction of marines on Koh Tang. The aircraft were from the 40th ARRS from Nakhon Phanom. Its three 7.62mm miniguns provided suppressing fire that frequently stopped the Cambodians from shooting down the helicopters around Koh Tang. (US Air Force)

Washington throughout the *Mayaguez* incident. The NMCC communicated through a JCS voice alert network, secure voice, and a secure teletypewriter message system. CINCPAC disseminated directives to Commander-in-Chief, PACFLT (CINCPACFLT) and 7AF's immediate headquarters, Commander-in-Chief, Pacific Air Forces (CINCPACAF). Although not in the direct operational chain of command, CINCPACAF had control of several support activities in the Philippines and he was still 7AF's commander. CINCPAC had its own secure voice and teletypewriter capabilities. Gayler's staff in Honolulu had a teletypewriter system to transmit written directives, but they also had access to a Defense Satellite Communications System capability to get instant contact with Burns.

COMUSSAG/7AF could direct all naval, air, and ground operations from his Nakhon Phanom headquarters. During the operation, Burns turned on-site command over to an EC-130 Airborne Battlefield, Communications, Command, and Control (ABCCC) aircraft circling in the vicinity. The

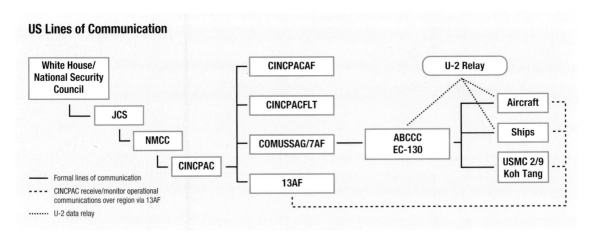

US Lines of Communication

White House/National Security Council — JCS — NMCC — CINCPAC

CINCPACAF
CINCPACFLT
COMUSSAG/7AF — ABCCC EC-130
13AF

U-2 Relay
Aircraft
Ships
USMC 2/9 Koh Tang

— Formal lines of communication
--- CINCPAC receive/monitor operational communications over region via 13AF
...... U-2 data relay

Fears that B-52D bombing might produce heavy civilian and collateral damage forced Washington to reconsider their use in Cambodia. Instead, *Coral Sea* tactical aircraft armed with precision guided munitions, like this Walleye bomb, had to make the attacks. These weapons gave CINCPAC more capability to hit specific targets. (US Navy)

EC-130 ABCCC was codenamed "Cricket," and its capabilities were critical to harmonizing the many simultaneous actions planned for May 15. A Cricket aircraft transmitted orders to all forces in theater, and its battle staff coordinated aircraft flights, deployments of forces, integrated requests for support, and other activities. Cricket talked to the marines through very high frequency (VHF), frequency modulation, and ultra high frequency (UHF) radio communications, while the EC-130 battle staff directed aircraft and ships mainly through a UHF radio link. A secondary system to support the ABCCC was a SAC U-2 aircraft, which served as a manual UHF relay and allowed Burns to communicate with any aircraft or ships in the area. COMUSSAG/7AF also could send and receive messages to CINCPACFLT ships via a high frequency secure teletypewriter. Unfortunately, staff ranging from CINCPAC to the White House could also listen to traffic and respond directly to any messages from deployed units in action.

A-6As, from the *Coral Sea's* CAW-15, participated in the attacks on the Cambodian coast. The A-6s pictured here are similar to the ones that hit Kompong Som and Ream. The aircraft had two crew members and could deliver ordnance with precision at night or under poor weather conditions. (US Navy)

THE RAID

The Khmer Rouge take action

While Ford and the NSC debated American military and diplomatic actions, the Khmer Rouge naval contingent that had taken the *Mayaguez* crew captive was also busy. From 1640hrs (all times are local Cambodian) to 1700hrs on May 13, they forced Miller and his crew onto two fishing boats and anchored near an East Beach cove. The *Mayaguez* remained in Cambodian hands, but the ship had no power. The fishing boats anchored about 76yd from shore, but no American left the boats. Some Khmer Rouge members did depart for Koh Tang.

A Cambodian interrogated Miller's crew. He wanted to know their mission and cargo. Miller explained that the ship carried neither guns nor munitions. He even proposed that his captors search the ship as proof. At about 2000hrs, Miller and another crew member accompanied several Cambodians back to the *Mayaguez* to search it. Miller never reached his ship, as an RF-4C appeared and dropped flares to illuminate then photograph the ship. The Cambodians, frightened by the aircraft, returned to the cove. Aircraft buzzed the island all night, and the defenders directed antiaircraft fire at these planes without success.

The shipping movements near Koh Tang had heightened US worries about the American crew being moved. That evening, the JCS ordered CINCPAC to authorize his aircraft to use riot control agent (RCA) tear gas munitions, bombs, and gunfire to stop the *Mayaguez* from reaching the mainland. Aircrews did not have to deploy any munitions, as the Khmer Rouge did not attempt to move the ship. A few hours later, CINCPAC received a NMCC message ordering Air Force and Navy assets to isolate Koh Tang; 7AF and PACFLT forces were to intercept any ships trying to enter or exit the area. Air Force pilots reported five boats in the area about 300yd offshore from Koh Tang.

The next day, a Khmer Rouge naval officer decided to take Miller and his shipmates to Kompong Som. Debate had raged

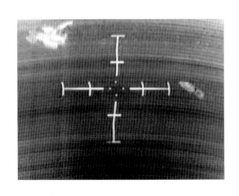

AC-130s used their sensors to illuminate targets. Here, an AC-130 has just engaged a Cambodian gunboat with 20mm and 40mm guns. USAF aircraft tried to isolate the Cambodians on Koh Tang to ensure that *Mayaguez* crew members were not transferred to the mainland nor Cambodian reinforcements could deploy to the island. (US Air Force)

between the Cambodian naval contingent, who wanted to keep the Americans on Koh Tang, and the Khmer Rouge island forces who wanted nothing to do with them. The Koh Tang garrison argued that it had no facilities to keep the sailors, not enough food, and controlling 40 prisoners would be a drain on the undermanned facility. The American crew had to go. An AC-130 crew spotted several boats leaving the Koh Tang area headed to the mainland at 0530hrs. The JCS' fear that the *Mayaguez*'s crew might head to the mainland came true. Ford had just approved the sinking of Cambodian ships trying to leave Koh Tang and the JCS issued the order. A-7D and other aircraft went into action.

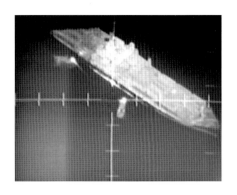

An AC-13 took this night shot of the *Mayaguez* before Miller and another crew member arrived with their Khmer Rouge captors. The Cambodians wanted to search the ship for arms and munitions, but an RF-4C, dropping flares, frightened them off. (US Air Force)

Eight minutes after Ford's decision, at 0720hrs, two A-7Ds dropped RCA sub-munitions on a Swift boat northeast of Koh Tang, trying to stop it. Failing to divert its course, the pilots fired 20mm rounds near the ship as warning shots, but struck it; the vessel caught fire and sank. A HH-53C helicopter tried to rescue the ten crew members, but it was not successful. After the A-7Ds destroyed the boat, a P-3 sighted a fishing boat with about 30–40 people huddled in the bow, described as "Caucasians," headed due north to Kompong Som. The boat was moving at about 5 knots. Several American aircraft subsequently saw the fishing boat, including four A-7Ds, two F-4s, a C-130, and a KC-135 tanker. The rationale for the marines taking Koh Tang had departed on the Thai fishing boat. Unfortunately, Washington was not sure that all of the crew had moved – NSA signals intelligence analysts intercepted a message that indicated some of the crew was still on Koh Tang – but the intelligence was inaccurate, and the whole crew had indeed departed.

The 7AF pilots tried several times to stop the boat. Fears of wounding or killing some of the people aboard forced the pilots to avoid direct fire on the ship. An F-4 fighter unleashed a 20mm burst across the boat's bow, and also used 2.75in rockets. These actions failed to turn the craft. F-111As then dropped bombs in an attempt to intimidate the Khmer Rouge crew, and A-7Ds also released RCA through CBU-30 (cluster bomb unit) sub-munitions at about 70ft above the fishing boat's stern. The pilots made several passes; the A-7Ds ejected CBU-30 sub-munitions many times. Captives and captors vomited due to the tear gas, but the fishing trawler chugged forward – armed Khmer Rouge guards forced the Thai crew, at gunpoint, to move towards the mainland despite the tear gas. The A-7Ds returned 30 minutes later and dropped RCA munitions again, but they failed to deter the vessel. A pilot offered to disable the ship by shooting out the rudder, but Washington declined. Ford was incensed that the military had allowed any Khmer Rouge ships to leave Koh Tang. While Jones and Schlesinger tried to get guidance from Ford, the President wanted to find out why the pilots did not follow his order. He later issued a directive to sink all boats in the area. Jones and others reminded the President that there could still be Americans on the boats, but Jones authorized tactical aircraft and naval gunfire attacks against all Cambodian small naval vessels within 25 nautical miles of Koh Tang,

This Cambodian Swift boat lies damaged near the East Beach. Although the craft could not move, Khmer Rouge sailors used its .50-caliber machine guns to thwart American efforts to reinforce marines on Koh Tang. The *Holt* eventually destroyed the boat with its 0.5in guns. (US Air Force)

Kompong Som, Poulo Wai, and Ream. These forces were not to attack into Vietnamese territory.

A-7D and RF-4C crews watched the fishing boat enter waters off Kompong Som. The boats anchored about a mile south of the harbor. The failure to stop the boat forced the President to move faster. He wanted to avoid any lengthy negotiation for their release, and a military action might convince the Cambodian leadership to release the crew.

Throughout May 14, the 7AF pilots observed patrol boats operating throughout the Koh Tang area. Aircraft attacked several patrol vessels, and F-4s sank two small craft between the *Mayaguez* and Koh Tang. An AC-130 aircraft also destroyed a patrol craft about 2 nautical miles east northeast of the island. Air Force crews damaged four other ships. During the night, AC-130s continued to attack patrol craft.

In the morning, Phnom Penh had received word about the *Mayaguez*'s capture, as the world press reported the incident. George H. W. Bush had tried to deliver the diplomatic demands to the Cambodian embassy in Beijing, but failed. The United Nations had attempted and failed to get Cambodia to acknowledge America's request to release the ship and its crew. Washington's "Voice of America" radio station broadcast demands to release the crew and the ship at 1800hrs Cambodian time. There was no response. The American military presence had also visibly intensified in the Gulf of Thailand. The local Cambodian naval commander who had seized the *Mayaguez* wanted the Kompong Som garrison to take control of the American ship's crew. The garrison commander refused to take anyone.

The naval officer had no other alternative but to leave. He took the crew to Koh Rong Sam Lem, a Cambodian naval compound about 10 nautical miles southwest of Kompong Som. An English-speaking Khmer Rouge naval officer questioned Miller again. The interrogator wanted to know if any crew members had CIA or Federal Bureau of Investigation (FBI) affiliation. He also inquired once again about the ship's cargo and mission. After consulting with his superiors, he then asked how Miller had contacted the aircraft that had sunk the Khmer Rouge patrol boats. The officer pressed Miller about how many men he needed to get his ship underway, and if he could contact the appropriate authorities to call off the air attacks. Miller convinced the Cambodian that if he and his crew returned to the *Mayaguez*, then he could contact the American military and stop the bombing. After discussions with Phnom Penh, the officer notified Miller that he and nine crew members would return to the ship and use the radio to call for a ceasefire. The notification came at 1300hrs; they would depart at dusk by a gunboat. However, the gunboat crew feared that they would be targets for American aircraft. Miller and the crew would remain overnight. During this time, Phnom Penh decided to release all of the crew and that they would all leave on a fishing boat at daybreak, at about the same time as the start of the Koh Tang assault and the *Mayaguez* seizure.

Unfortunately, Ford and the NSC did not know about this decision. Other events also shaped the final call to launch the American rescue. The

MAY 15
1975

0542hrs
Planned
operational start
time for
Koh Tang assault

Cambodians had detained a Thai freighter for two hours just 30 miles east of where they had taken the *Mayaguez*, and Khmer Rouge gunboats had also fired upon the *Hirado*, a Swedish refrigerator cargo ship. The American embassy in Tehran, Iran, had reported that a senior Chinese diplomat mentioned that his government was trying to influence the Cambodians to release the crew. The diplomat believed that the *Mayaguez* crew would soon be free. Kissinger received this report, but did not report the news to Ford. The American assault force now had only a few hours before the attack.

Under the War Powers Resolution, Ford gave notification to congressional members about his proposed actions. On the afternoon of May 14, the Senate Foreign Relations Committee drafted and passed unanimously a resolution that condemned Cambodia for taking the *Mayaguez* and noted the President's attempts to use diplomatic means to solve the situation. The committee also voted to support Ford to exercise his constitutional powers to release the crew.

With no apparent success with the United Nations, the American demands for the crew and ship's release, Ford started to issue operational orders. Around 1645hrs on May 14 (Washington time), Ford told Jones to relay the order to take the *Mayaguez*, assault Koh Tang, and begin the air raids. In Thailand, USAF helicopter crews were getting ready to transport the marines; it was 0345hrs on May 15. Jones transmitted the orders by voice to CINCPAC. He also confirmed Ford's directives to seize and secure the *Mayaguez* and to conduct the helicopter assault on Koh Tang. PACFLT would launch *Coral Sea* aircraft against Kompong Som at 0745hrs. Jones specifically mentioned not to attack any merchant ships in the harbor unless they could be identified. The aircraft pilots had to make maximum use of PGMs.

The JCS and CINCPAC staffs were moving towards military actions. The *Coral Sea* was now within seven hours of its destination, although it was already in aircraft range and could conduct flight operations. The *Holt* also reported that it was ready to receive the marines to board the *Mayaguez*.

America responds

The US forces were ready to initiate offensive actions to take back the *Mayaguez* and its crew. The USAF had already sunk Khmer Rouge ships, now 7AF was preparing to support the assault. More importantly, helicopter crews started preflight activities for the missions to Koh Tang and the *Holt*. Likewise, the BLT 1/4 and 2/9 Marines received final briefings and loaded ammunition, supplies, and weapons onto the helicopters. The *Wilson* and the *Holt* were getting prepared to receive the boarding party and to shield the area from any possible Khmer Rouge gunboat interference. Washington was ready to act.

The HH-53C and CH-53C aircraft scheduled to fly out over the Gulf of Thailand had few veteran crews. Most of the pilots and co-pilots had not served in the Vietnam War, but had participated in Operations *Frequent Wind* and *Eagle Pull*. Fortunately, some of the pararescue and flight engineers were experienced, combat noncommissioned

**MAY 15
1975**

**0600hrs
Marines commence
landings on
Koh Tang**

The *Holt*'s commander was concerned about enemy gunboats or craft attacking amidships – the 5in main gun and other weapons did not have to ability to protect the ship in those areas. Navy crews armed with M-60s, M-16s, and other small arms guarded the ship from gunboats while marines boarded the *Mayaguez*. (US Navy)

Commander Peterson successfully positioned his ship near the *Mayaguez* with one attempt. He did not know if the difference in deck height would affect the seizure. This photograph indicates that the concern was unfounded. Note the relative size of the *Holt* to the *Mayaguez*. (US Navy)

officers (NCOs). The helicopter crews did not have much training with other services. Rescue and special operations activities did not typically involve the particular tactical maneuvers and approaches needed for a helicopter assault on an island or ship, especially if operations occurred under fire. These helicopters also did not normally fly in formation, unless they were trying to refuel in flight.

The helicopters flown by the USAF and the assault helicopters used by the marines were similar. Different missions forced some distinct changes in configuration. The HH-53C had more armor plating to protect the crew during rescue missions than a typical CH-53C. Normal missions of CH-53s in 21st SOS service included delivery and extraction of personnel in enemy-held territory. The CH-53C had to carry personnel and equipment over longer distances, and crews could trade this payload for the removal of some of the armor plating. The HH-53C also had an aerial refueling boom that could extend the range of the helicopter or allow it to stay over an area for an extended time to search for downed aircrews. Armament was also different: the 40th ARRS HH-53 aircrews operated three 7.62mm miniguns compared to only two in the CH-53C. Both helicopter types carried two external fuel tanks. The HH-53C's tanks contained 450 gallons of fuel, but they also featured a fire-retardant polyurethane foam system that would limit damage to the aircraft if hit by enemy gunfire. The CH-53C carried two 650-gallon tanks to compensate for its lack of aerial refueling capability, but did not have the fire-retardant system. Several 21st SOS personnel had requested the same fire-retardant system for the CH-53C fuel tanks, but CINCPACAF did not give approval. The 40th ARRS used the call sign "Jolly Green" for their HH-53Cs, while the CH-53Cs responded to "Knife."

With marines loaded aboard, 11 helicopters left U-Tapao for the *Holt* and Koh Tang. The pilots took off from 0414hrs to 0425hrs and flew in loose formation on a southwesterly course into the Gulf of Thailand.

Recovering the *Mayaguez*: "Marines over the side"

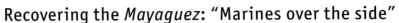

Major Ray E. Porter, 1/4 Marines' executive officer, and Captain Walt Wood's force were in three HH-53Cs: Jolly Green (JG) 11, 12, and 13. By 0600hrs, the first helicopter had reached the *Holt*. The destroyer escort's small antisubmarine helicopter pad, used by its antisubmarine SH-2 Seasprite, did not provide room to land a HH-53C. The helicopter pilot also had to ensure the main rotor would not hit any part of the ship. The only option to offload the marines was to set down the front landing gear on the pad and have the passengers depart from the one of the front crew doors. The operation went smoothly with all personnel on the *Holt* within 15–20 minutes. The three helicopters had brought the 48-man contingent from Company D, the MSC personnel, and the Navy volunteers to power up the *Mayaguez*, two Air Force EOD technicians, and an Army linguist. The MSC

civilian personnel had come from the USNS *Greenville Victory*, a World War II-era cargo ship. The Navy personnel from the USS *Duluth*, an *Austin*-class amphibious transport ship, had just finished recovering refugees from Operation *Frequent Wind*. JG11 and 12 returned to Thailand to prepare for the second wave assault on Koh Tang. JG13 remained near the action to help in any search-and-rescue effort. Commander Robert Peterson, the *Holt*'s captain, got the ship moving at 25 knots towards the *Mayaguez* at 0630hrs.

While Wood conducted preparations to board the container ship, the Khmer Rouge on Koh Rong Sam Lem freed the *Mayaguez* crew. Miller and his men received final approval from Phnom Penh to return to their ship at about 0620hrs. Six Khmer Rouge sailors accompanied Miller onto a Thai fishing boat. Twenty minutes after leaving Koh Rong Sam Lem, another fishing boat intercepted the Thai vessel. The Cambodian captors left the Thai boat and told the American crew that they could return to the

OPPOSITE, BOTTOM: Arms at the ready. This marine prepares to go aboard the *Mayaguez* from the *Holt*. With gas mask on, he prepares for the worst. A-7Ds delivered riot control agents onto the container ship to incapacitate any Khmer Rouge defenders. Fortunately, no one was killed or wounded during the boarding. (US Navy)

AMERICA'S SPEAR POINT: THE UNITED STATES MARINE CORPS

The Vietnam War's end in 1975 meant a return to normal training duty for the USMC. Marine units throughout the Pacific prepared for an unpredictable future, with duties ranging from embassy security details, Fleet Marine Pacific deployments, guarding naval installations and ships, and acting as a ready force. The marine units also had to respond at a moment's notice to any national emergency, like the *Mayaguez* incident.

Within hours of the *Mayaguez* alert, marine officers had to send men and material from the Philippines and Okinawa to get ready to board a ship and potentially assault an unknown location. Sketchy conditions forced officers to plan with broad concepts. With no time to train or coordinate with Navy, USAF, and other participants, the officers from 1/4 and 2/9 Marines had to make do with their limited resources to execute a unique raid under constantly changing conditions.

Layers of decision makers, some in theater and others in Washington, debated tactical decisions that affected the final concepts. Officers in the field had to improvise and overcome problems, a trademark of the Marine Corps. One example stands out. During the final planning phase for the *Mayaguez* boarding and Koh Tang assault, COMUSSAG/7AF and the *Mayaguez* ground security force commander, Colonel Johnson, had agreed to a direct helicopter assault on the container ship. CINCPACFLT had disagreed and pushed the concept of helicopters transporting the marines to the *Holt*, which would then transfer them to the *Mayaguez*. Since COMMUSSAG/7AF did not control PACFLT assets in the

area, the decision had to go to CINCPAC. The plan that Admiral Gayler reviewed had inadvertently specified a direct helicopter insertion on the *Mayaguez*. Gayler found the CINCPACFLT concept less risky and approved the plan with that modification. Johnson had only a few hours to design and coordinate a new plan. Fortunately, the ship seizure occurred without any problems.

Marines in Subic Bay, Philippines, also reacted swiftly when CINCPAC activated the 9th Marine Amphibious Brigade (9 MAB) to support the *Mayaguez* operations. The 9 MAB's commander put together a staff at 0800hrs on May 13. The 2/4 Marines served as the ground element with 662 men. CH-53s from Heavy Marine Helicopter Squadron 462 (HMH-462) would provide direct support. The marines could also count on CH-46s to land forces and conduct resupply missions. The 9 MAB personnel and equipment started to load onto the *Hancock* and the *Mobile* within hours. Their potential missions included taking Poulo Wai, occupying Kompong Som, landing on Koh Tang, and seizing the *Mayaguez*. The task force left Subic Bay at 0700hrs the next day. While 9 MAB staff monitored the Air Force Command Net for information, the marines heard about the 7AF helicopter rescue of the Koh Tang assault force. The planning for combat operations turned to a rescue mission. The 2/4 and HMH-462 marines stood ready in case the USAF helicopters failed. Fortunately, the extraction took place within hours. Still, 9 MAB was ready to execute an attack on Kompong Som. CINCPAC deactivated the task force on May 18.

**MAY 15
1975**

**0725–0822hrs
Marines board
and clear the
*Mayaguez***

Marines swarm throughout the *Mayaguez*. It took a little more than an hour to secure the ship. Company D was involved in the first naval hostile ship-to-ship boarding since 1826. The marines accomplished the recovery without a hitch, unlike the Koh Tang assault. (US Navy)

Mayaguez. Earlier, the Cambodian guards had given Miller's crew long bamboo poles, to which they tied some white undershirts to ward off attacks by any American combat aircraft or naval ships. At 0607hrs, Hu Nim, Cambodian Minister of Information and Propaganda, made a domestic 19-minute radio broadcast. He stated Phnom Penh's willingness to release the *Mayaguez* and allow it to leave Cambodian waters. The broadcast made no specific mention of the crew. Kissinger did not inform Ford about the message until 0715hrs.

Peterson and Wood were ready to take the *Mayaguez*. Peterson was now only 10–15 minutes from his target and called for the RCA drop. Three A-7Ds delivered the RCA with 16 CBU-30s over the freighter at 0719hrs. Peterson then carefully maneuvered the *Holt* for the boarding. The destroyer escort had only one propeller screw, but moved the vessel so that he would allow the marines to enter the ship from his portside. At about 200yd from the *Mayaguez*, Peterson called in the strafing run, but later waved it off since they were closing too fast. Marines and sailors watched for any Khmer Rouge defenders, but none showed.

One of Peterson's major concerns was how to board the ship. The *Holt* would come alongside the container ship, but differences in deck heights might make a boarding difficult. Fortunately, the main decks were about the same height. With the *Holt* next to the *Mayaguez*, Lieutenant Commander John Todd, Peterson's executive officer, ordered "Marines over the side." With gas masks on, Wood and Corporal C. R. Coker jumped onto the *Mayaguez* at 0725hrs, to begin securing the vessel. Coker moved towards the bridge. A squad was supposed to follow the two men onto the freighter, but the ships drifted apart by about 25ft and the remaining boarding party could not come cross the gap. The captain and the corporal quickly secured the ships together once they retrieved mooring lines from the *Holt*.

Now, with the ships tied together, two marine squads started to search the freighter. A squad took control of the bridge. Another moved below decks towards its objective, the engine room. Other personnel started to look for any Khmer Rouge soldiers and booby traps. The EOD team found no bombs or mines. The marines on the *Mayaguez*'s bridge did find evidence of the Cambodians, in the form of prepared food, but the Khmer Rouge detail had apparently abandoned ship. At 0822hrs, the *Holt* signaled to CINPAC that the ship was secure. Porter and Wood raised the American flag on the *Mayaguez* at 0825hrs. While the MSC and naval personnel started to get the *Mayaguez* under steam, the *Holt* prepared to tow the freighter. Leaving a small marine contingent onboard, Wood and the remaining marines returned to the *Holt*. They were prepared to support the Koh Tang assault as a contingency. Two oceanic tugs had also headed towards the *Mayaguez* to get it into international waters if the crew failed to get the freighter under steam, but were not needed. Once underway, the *Holt* could turn to other combat operations near Koh Tang.

While the marines were taking the *Mayaguez*, Miller and his crew churned towards Koh Tang. The *Wilson* was on station by 0710hrs. The air raids on Kompong Som and Ream also began. More importantly, the helicopter assault on Koh Tang had started. Ford released an announcement to the Cambodians, at 0815hrs, that if they would release the crew unconditionally and immediately, then he would order all military operations to cease. The White House also mentioned that Americans had retaken the *Mayaguez*.

A controller on the EC-130 Cricket aircraft received a report that a small craft had appeared, headed from the Kompong Som area to Koh Tang. A P-3 investigated. The pilot reported at 0935hrs that the boat, some 13 nautical miles from Koh Tang, had about 30 Caucasians on board waving white flags. The *Wilson* got underway and intercepted the ship. Initial

Marines retook the *Mayaguez* with little opposition. Still, fear of mines or sabotage by the Khmer Rouge forced American military and civilian personnel to search the containers, superstructure, and engine room carefully. They found no booby traps or explosive devices. The ship was ready to get underway in hours. (US Navy)

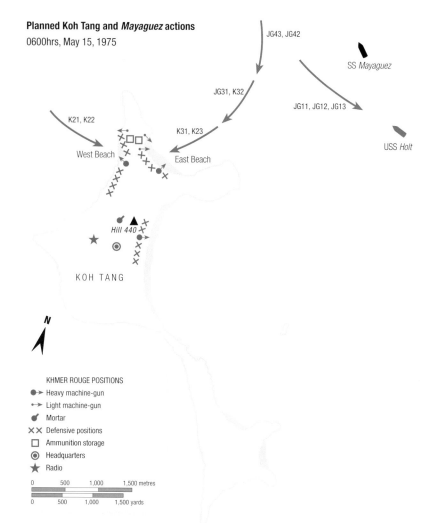

Planned Koh Tang and *Mayaguez* actions
0600hrs, May 15, 1975

JG43, JG42

SS *Mayaguez*

JG31, K32

JG11, JG12, JG13

K21, K22

K31, K23

USS *Holt*

West Beach

East Beach

Hill 440

KOH TANG

N

KHMER ROUGE POSITIONS
●➤ Heavy machine-gun
➤ Light machine-gun
🔥 Mortar
✕✕ Defensive positions
☐ Ammunition storage
◉ Headquarters
★ Radio

0   500   1,000   1,500 metres
0   500   1,000   1,500 yards

**MAY 15
1975**

**1040hrs
Mayaguez crew
released**

The *Holt*'s bridge was busy during the boarding of the freighter. Commander Peterson, the *Holt*'s captain, is at the center of the photograph. The frigate was ready to take action if Cambodian defenders decided to contest the boarding. Fortunately, the *Mayaguez* was abandoned and the mission uneventful. (US Navy)

reports from the *Wilson* indicated that only 30 of the 40 crew were on the boat, but staff quickly corrected the report – all 40 of the *Mayaguez* crew and five Thai sailors were recovered. Burns' headquarters sent a message, copying in the White House, confirming the release of the crew at 1040hrs. The Thais received food and fuel, and told the Americans that the Cambodians had held them for five months. They then left for home. America had now recovered the ship and crew. The *Wilson* headed to the *Mayaguez* to return the crew. At 1045hrs, the *Wilson*'s captain told the JCS that Miller had convinced the Cambodians that if they were released, the Americans would stop any airstrikes. Ford made a public announcement that the Cambodians had released the crew and ship at 1127hrs, but air operations continued.

Miller and his crew returned to the *Mayaguez* at 1205hrs. The *Holt* had taken the freighter under tow and it headed north of Koh Tang towards Thailand. When the *Mayaguez* came under steam, Peterson ordered the tow line cut. The *Holt* had escorted the container ship until it was 12 nautical miles from any Cambodian territory, in what Phnom Penh classified as international waters. Unfortunately, Peterson could not retrieve any of the MSC, Navy, Marine, or other personnel, since CINCPAC ordered them to support the marines at Koh Tang immediately.

Green Lizards, Fighting Redcocks, and Mighty Shrikes go to war

The *Coral Sea* was ready for action by the morning of May 15. Rear Admiral R. P. Coogan, commanding Task Force 77 (TF 77), had his carrier

air wing prepared for the first mission, an armed reconnaissance flight over the targeted area. The carrier air wing on the *Coral Sea* consisted of five tactical air squadrons plus several detachments. VF-51 (Screaming Eagles) and VF-111 (Sundowners) flew F-4N Phantom II fighters that provided combat air patrols over the targeted areas. The F-4N pilots could also strafe and bomb ground targets. The primary attack capability came from VA-95 (Green Lizards), VA-22 (Fighting Redcocks), and VA-94 (Mighty Shrikes). The Green Lizards had a mix of A-6A Intruder bombers and KA-6D tankers. The Fighting Redcocks and Mighty Shrikes operated the single seated A-7E Corsair II. TF-77 also had its own E-1B airborne early warning aircraft, RF-8G photo-reconnaissance jets, and SH-3G rescue helicopters. The wing had come aboard the aircraft carrier in December 1974. This day would provide the pilots with their first and only combat mission of their seven-month western Pacific cruise.

Coogan had launched his aircraft at 0705hrs to ensure he met the planned time over target (TOT) at 0745hrs. The Navy pilots' mission was to locate and identify any boats or aircraft in the area. If identified as Cambodian, they could attack. Coogan estimated that he could launch an aircraft strike every one hour and 15 minutes to achieve his objectives.

Before the air strikes, Ford and the NSC were in a quandary. The President had received reports that the Cambodians had released the *Mayaguez*, but had no news of the crew. At 0728hrs, Ford ordered TF 77 pilots not to drop any ordnance over Kompong Som. Discussions between CINCPAC and the NMCC revolved around the impact of the Cambodian announcement on the mission. Confusion set in. Orders from the White House at 0729hrs then directed CINCPAC not to launch the *Coral Sea*'s aircraft against Kompong Som. Five minutes later, the JCS staff sent a verbal message to CINCPAC to use all communications means to divert and cancel the first mission. By 0744hrs, the JCS cancelled all of the cyclic air strike missions on the mainland, one minute before TOT for the *Coral Sea* aircraft. Four minutes later, another order from the NMCC restored the first attack mission to hit the Cambodian mainland and conduct battle damage assessment (BDA). They provided no rationale. Scowcroft approved all of the scheduled cyclic missions again. The NMCC transmitted his message to continue the bombing as planned. A 0757hrs PACFLT message confirmed the directive to resume attacks on the Cambodian mainland. Flying crews, planners, maintenance teams, and flight deck personnel had to adjust and prepare for the upcoming missions. The *Coral Sea*'s aircraft barely reached the Cambodian coast. The armed reconnaissance mission returned to the *Coral Sea* at 0830hrs. Although the pilots did not use their weapons, they did identify an oil refinery in the Kompong Som area as a potential target.

TF 77 aircraft prepared for the planned second wave. At 0845hrs, the *Coral Sea* launched two A-6A and five A-7E attack jets along with support planes to attack the Ream airfield. This wave stuck at 0957hrs. RF-4C aircraft had photographed the airfield and analysts found aircraft were present. The A-6A and A-7E jets destroyed two C-47s and a C-46. The Navy pilots left two aircraft damaged. Initial pilot BDA reports indicated as many as 17 aircraft destroyed, but the pilots had overestimated the damage. After the attack, photo-reconnaissance analysts counted only 12 aircraft at the Ream airfield. The speed of the aircraft and the minimum 6,000ft altitude may have affected the reporting. The Navy pilots did, however, crater the Ream runway. The aircrews also bombed and strafed a petroleum, oil, and lubricant (POL) storage facility, warehouses, a 37mm antiaircraft artillery site, and hangers. The aircrews reported a large POL fire and they had damaged the 37mm gun position.

The Thai-based fishing boat used to carry Miller to the *Wilson* was also the same vessel that took him and his crew to Koh Rong Sam Lem from Koh Tang via Kompong Som. The Cambodians captured and held the Thai crew for five months. One can see the *Mayaguez* towed by the *Holt* in the top right. (US Navy)

OPPOSITE, BOTTOM: The marines found evidence of previous Cambodian presence on the *Mayaguez*. Prepared food, cold and uneaten, was on the bridge. Khmer Rouge sailors had left the ship unmanned. The American military party that took control of the ship did not find any weapons; allegedly, $5,000 in cash went missing from the captain's cabin. (US Navy)

The marines who took the *Mayaguez* were well armed with M-16s, shotguns, M-79 grenade launchers, M-60 machine guns, and other weapons. These marines could only watch as activities heated up on Koh Tang island, in the background. There was consideration of landing the marines via *Holt's* gig, but no one requested it. (US Navy)

At 1020hrs, Coogan launched the third wave. While the aircraft were in flight to the targets, CINCPAC was made aware that a condition of the *Mayaguez* crew's release was a cessation of aircraft attacks. Gayler asked Jones if the third planned attack should continue. Schlesinger authorized the third wave, and Jones notified CINCPAC to proceed. The strike force had several targets: Kompong Som's harbor, the Phumi Phsar Ream naval base, and the POL refinery north of Kompong Som identified by the first mission. Before each mission, TF 77 sent a list of targets to the JCS. IPAC did not propose the POL refinery target to Coogan, since intelligence center personnel knew that the refinery had been non-operational for years. At 1050hrs, the bombing began. Two A-6A and two A-7E planes hit the Ream naval facility, destroying a barrack and causing fires at a POL storage area. Four A-7Es set two warehouses on fire, causing moderate structural damage, and scored a direct hit on a railroad marshalling yard building, probably a warehouse, near Kompong Som. The aircraft also hit the POL refinery target identified from the first mission. Pilots damaged and holed some storage tanks, but nothing was set aflame.

The final bombing mission prepared for action. The strike force of two A-6As, four A-7Es, and escorting F-4N aircraft left the *Coral Sea* at 1145hrs. TF 77 moved south of Koh Tang, the ships now about 85–90 nautical miles from the island. While the *Coral Sea* aircraft sped towards their targets, Schlesinger had decided, with the JCS' recommendation, to cancel the mission. The strike aircraft did not hit any targets, but an A-7E did sink a patrol boat 5 nautical miles south of the island. The last *Coral Sea* pilot returned to the aircraft carrier at 1335hrs.

The Green Lizards, Fighting Redcocks, and Mighty Shrikes completed their missions, a total of 15 sorties. Green Lizard tankers also made six sorties. TF 77 pilots conducted two E-1B sorties and another two RF-8G missions on May 15 to support the attacks. Coogan could now focus on Koh Tang.

Koh Tang: A costly initial assault

Before events clarified the situation, Ford, the NSC, CINCPAC, and others had evidence that the main focus of the rescue, the *Mayaguez* crew, might not be on Koh Tang. The fishing boat carrying a number of people, who looked like American crew members, to Kompong Som caused Washington to think twice. Was the assault on Koh Tang a reasonable mission? Did the Cambodians send the entire crew to the mainland? There was no conclusive proof to indicate that the Khmer Rouge had moved all 40 *Mayaguez* sailors to Kompong Som. After Captain Wood and his marines had secured the freighter, the CINCPAC staff had received a Cambodian radio transmission from an unknown location. The transmission mentioned, "Let the Americans go.

We do not want to become prisoners ourselves." Intelligence analysts could only speculate if the message was from Phnom Penh to Koh Tang or Kompong Som. Washington and Honolulu could not discount the idea that the Khmer Rouge was holding American prisoners on the island early on May 15.

CINCPAC had put into play a number of actions that required precise timing and simultaneous activities. The *Mayaguez* seizure, TF 77 and the *Coral Sea* aircraft strikes on Cambodia, and BLT 2/9's helicopter assault and search of Koh Tang were scheduled to occur about the same time. Jones, Gayler, and Burns had already set actions into motion. Stopping the helicopter attack on Koh Tang might be possible, but they were almost ready to hit the beaches.

Elements of BLT 2/9 had departed with 1/4's Company D from U-Tapao at 0415hrs. Unfortunately, Phnom Penh's 0607hrs radio broadcast about the Khmer Rouge willingness to release the container ship occurred after the HH-53C and CH-53C had left Thailand. While the marines approached Koh Tang, American intelligence analysts had just translated the message. Even if the message reached Ford, the marines would have already touched down on the East and West Beaches.

The marines who landed on the *Mayaguez* had moved from the Philippines, Thailand, and onto the *Holt* within a short time. Still, they performed very well under the circumstances and retook the ship without any practice and against a potentially hostile Khmer Rouge force with AK-47s, RPGs, and machine guns. (US Navy)

The marine assault force nearing Koh Tang would land in pairs of helicopters. One pair, Knife (K)21 and 22, with parts of Company G including its commander Captain James H. Davis, approached the West Beach. K21 and K22's landing had to hit at first light to achieve surprise. At the same time, K23 and K31, carrying further elements of Company G, would strike the East Beach. Austin, with further units of BLT 2/9 in four other helicopters, was in the initial wave that would land on the East Beach too.

As the assault force flew close to Koh Tang, the sun's light appeared on the horizon, making the helicopters visible. Some of the helicopters had seen gunfire, probably from patrolling gunboats, but none from the shoreline. After the landings, the marines could call on five flights of A-7Ds for close air support, but it looked unnecessary now. The first wave would have no preparatory fires, naval or aerial, to hit any possible beach defenses. Besides, the *Holt* was busy with the *Mayaguez* and the *Wilson* would approach Koh Tang at about 0700hrs. Austin's mission was to search for and recover Miller and his crew. Any air bombardment or naval gunfire could accidently kill some of the *Mayaguez* crew. The marines only expected little resistance anyway.

The next pair, JG41 and K32 was only a mile back from K23 and K31. The last pair, JG42 and JG43, brought up the rear. The men on the East Beach were the main strike force to drive west towards the fishing village and link up with Davis' contingent.

At about 0600hrs, the helicopters approached the beaches. To offload the marines, the helicopter crews had to use their rear cargo ramp. A pilot had to turn the helicopter around to drop the rear ramp, putting the aircraft in a vulnerable position. Any enemy fire from the beaches would endanger the landings. Supporting American gunfire would have to come from the

Marines, onboard the recaptured *Mayaguez,* watch the *Wilson* sail by with Koh Tang in the background. The *Wilson* would get a radio call from a passing P-3 that reported a boat headed south to Koh Tang. It was a Thai fishing boat containing the released *Mayaguez* crew returning to their ship. (US Navy)

helicopters themselves – as one helicopter delivered its men, the other could provide fire support with its miniguns in an emergency. The CH-53C helicopters only had miniguns in the forward area of the aircraft; unlike the HH-53Cs, there was no minigun in the rear cargo ramp.

K21 started to unload the 20 marines onto the beach. Second Lieutenant James McDaniel had half of the 1st Platoon of Company G with him. The Cambodians, from their entrenched defensive positions, delivered immediate fire from AK-47s, RPGs, mortars, and machine guns. K22 tried to provide fire support; it reported a "Hot LZ" (landing zone) to Cricket at about 0605hrs. Air Force Captain Terry Ohlemeier, in K22, noted the shore "looked like a string of Christmas tree lights." Enemy gunfire damaged one of K21's engines and it had to leave the West Beach immediately. With the helicopter leaking fuel and emitting smoke, its pilot Lieutenant Colonel John Denham tried to control the CH-53C, but failed. Denham was the 21st SOS commander and had led the eight helicopters from U-Tapao to Koh Tang. As the crippled CH-53C struggled to stay airborne, the crew lightened the helicopter by ditching equipment and other items. The helicopter slid into the ocean, about three-quarters of a mile off the beach. Crew members started to evacuate the sinking CH-53C. All but one member escaped, Staff Sergeant Elwood Rumbaugh, the flight mechanic. Rumbaugh had helped the co-pilot get out the helicopter, but the crew never saw him again. He presumably drowned. Another USAF helicopter later rescued Denham and the rest of the crew.

Like K21, K22 was struck by many rounds, which produced fuel leaks and ripped up the airframe, and wounded marines in the cargo bay. Davis, in K22, could not join his men on the beach. Ohlemeier had problems controlling the helicopter. He had to abort the mission and try to fly back to Thailand. Losing altitude, power, and fuel, the K22 crew wondered if they could make landfall. Fortunately, the helicopter found a landing spot, about 83 nautical miles from U-Tapao. With the damaged instruments, the pilot was unsure of where they had set down – fear that they had landed in Cambodia was on the minds of the Air Force crew and the marines. Fortunately, JG11 and 12, returning from the *Holt*, linked up with K22 in flight. The damaged helicopter had landed in Thailand and JG12 returned the marines and their equipment to U-Tapao.

The West Beach assault had landed in a hornet's nest. The assault force suffered one helicopter destroyed and another damaged. McDaniel and his men had to contend with an enemy force much larger and more heavily armed than expected, and in good defensive positions. He did manage to move past the tree line and overrun a 60mm mortar position. The loss of helicopters also called into question the ability to send in more marines in the subsequent planned waves, and to resupply the force with critical ammunition and water.

If the marine assault in the western approach faced difficulties, the East Beach landing would prove even worse. K23 approached the beach. The gunfire on the West Beach had already erupted, so the Khmer Rouge defenders were ready. K23 took immediate fire as the marines from Company G's 3rd Platoon left the cargo bay. The helicopter's engine was dying and Cambodian RPG gunners shot off the rear tail section. K23's pilot had to set down his chopper a few hundred yards from shore, damaged beyond control. The pilot put the CH-53C into the water and the helicopter quickly flooded. With the rear cargo ramp down, the marines started to exit the downed chopper while firing into the tree line with M-16s. Second Lieutenant Michael Cicere, 3rd Platoon's commander, led his men towards the beach. The K23 crew and some Air Force personnel also disembarked, but the pilot and two others stayed behind to shut down the CH-53C and try to contact Cricket. When the three attempted to reach Cicere and the others, they came under fire. A flight mechanic was wounded, but all managed to reunite with the group.

K31 was trying to suppress the Cambodians from attacking K23, using one of its 7.62mm miniguns, but it also came under accurate gunfire. As K23 settled into the water, the Cambodians increasingly concentrated on taking down K31. The helicopter was on its final approach when it received a blast of heavy automatic gunfire and RPG volleys. One RPG struck the helicopter on the left side, wounding several men and igniting leaking fuel. One of the 650-gallon external fuel tanks exploded. The pilot, Major Howard Corson, tried to turn the helicopter around, but it was a fireball. K31's co-pilot, Second Lieutenant Richard Vandegeer, tried to use an M-16 to return fire from the cockpit while the helicopter moved away from the shore. Unfortunately, another RPG round stuck the cockpit, ripping out the instrument panel and wounding Vandegeer. Corson was in trouble – he was in danger of the Khmer Rouge shooting the CH-53C out of the skies. He had to set the helicopter down into the surf south of K23.

The *Mayaguez* boarding team tried to get the freighter quickly up to steam, but it took a few hours. The *Holt* towed the ship out to international waters; the Cambodian government recognized such waters 12 miles from its coastline. After reaching this limit, the *Holt* returned to Koh Tang. (US Navy)

The USS *Coral Sea*'s Carrier Air Wing-15 conducted several air raids on the Kompong Som area to punish the Cambodian government and stop any reinforcements moving to Koh Tang. An attack on the Ream airfield netted the destruction of three aircraft, including this C-47, although the raid failed to destroy any combat aircraft. (US Air Force)

THE ORIGINAL PLAN

Operations against SS *Mayaguez*, Koh Tang, and Cambodian mainland

KOH TANG ASSAULT 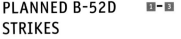 AND *MAYAGUEZ* BOARDING

1 First Wave: BLT 2/9 Company G, with 177 personnel, hits West Beach and East Beach. Helicopters will deliver 1/4 Company D marines to the *Holt* to form the boarding party.

2 Second Wave: BLT 2/9 Company E lands on East Beach.

3 Third wave: After Third Wave, CINCPAC has 650 personnel on Koh Tang.

PLANNED B-52D STRIKES

1 Cell 1: Three B-52Ds hit Phumi Phsar Ream naval base

2 Cell 2: Three B-52Ds hit Ream airfield

3 Cells 3 and 4: Six B-52Ds hit Kompong Som harbor

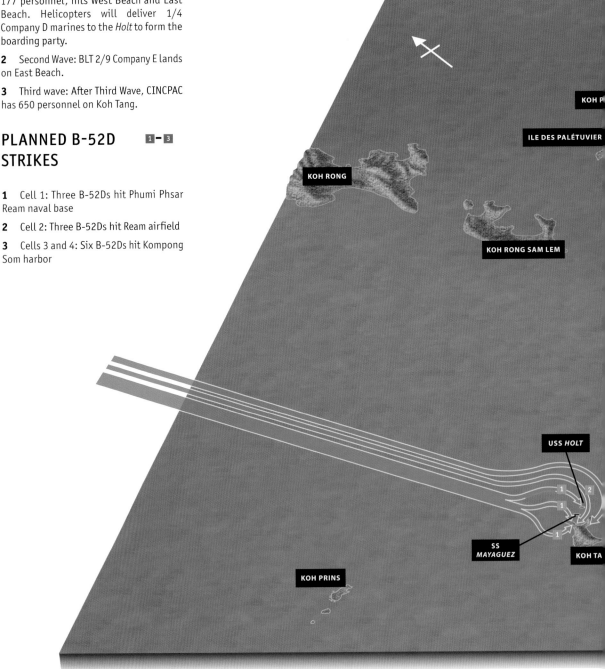

KEY

← Proposed B-52D operations

← Approved US movements

CARRIER STRIKE BY USS *CORAL SEA* ▫

1 Tactical aviation using precision-guided munitions (PGMs) can strike the same targets as the B-52Ds. NSC debates which force will hit Kompong Som and Ream. Withdrawal route after the attack

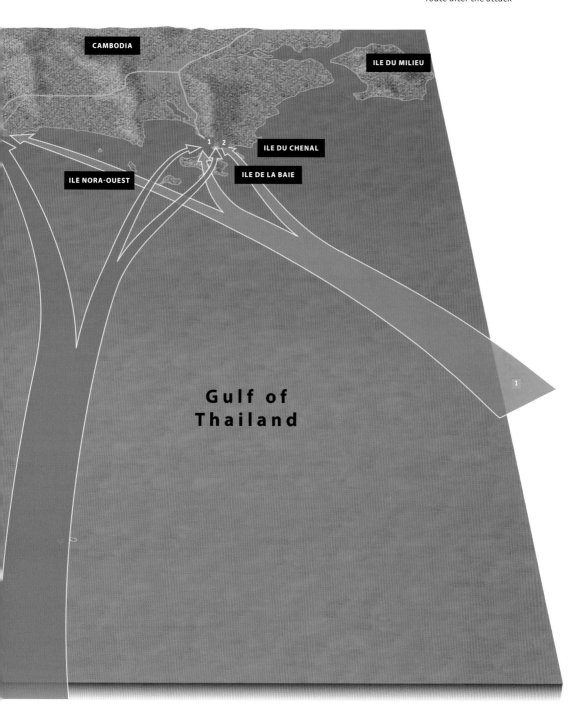

CAMBODIA

ILE DU MILIEU

ILE DU CHENAL

ILE DE LA BAIE

ILE NORA-OUEST

Gulf of Thailand

A 7.62mm minigun view of Koh Tang offers a good perspective of the terrain. Cambodian defensive works stymied efforts to land, reinforce, and evacuate the marines on Koh Tang. CH-53C and HH-53C miniguns proved invaluable in providing fire support all day and into the night. (US Air Force)

The only way to drop off or embark marines and other personnel on Koh Tang was through the rear cargo ramp. This HH-53C had the added advantage of a rear-mounted minigun. The gunner could therefore give some covering fire against Cambodians trying to shoot at the helicopter or passengers. (US Air Force)

K31's crew and the marines floated off Koh Tang. Although they were only in 4ft of water, they were vulnerable targets to the Cambodians. Air Force crews and marines performed heroically by helping rescue the wounded and assisting others escape the burning helicopter. Khmer Rouge gunfire had caused several casualties. Three marines who escaped the burning helicopter tried to storm the beach, but Cambodian soldiers easily cut them down. Ten marines, two Navy corpsmen, and Vandegeer died in the helicopter. Facing enemy fire, the survivors, some badly wounded or burned, started to head towards the Gulf of Thailand.

The survivors included Corson, two Air Force crew members, and ten marines. One of the marines, Lieutenant Terry Tonkin, was a critical asset to the BLT 2/9 force. He was the marine FAC officer who could direct air and naval gunfire support to the ground forces on Koh Tang. Unfortunately, all of his radio equipment was in K31. Despite the problems, Tonkin would provide help to his fellow marines on the beach. He used Corson's Air Force survival radio to contact Cricket. Tonkin directed A-7D close air support strafing missions against the Cambodian positions. Other A-7Ds tried to help McDaniel on the West Beach. Yet without marking smoke or any discernable landmarks, trying to establish positions to bomb or strafe was difficult.

Fortunately, for the K31 survivors, the *Wilson* was transiting the area. From about 1,000yd from the northeast tip of Koh Tang, spotters on the *Wilson* located K31 survivors, who were in three groups. The survivors had been in the water for a few hours by this time. The only way to rescue the men was by the *Wilson*'s gig, Black Velvet-1. Armed with two M-60 machine guns to return fire from any Cambodian attackers, the gig rescued two of the groups, while the *Wilson* picked up the third group. With the marines and Air Force crew secured and treated for their wounds, the *Wilson* proceeded north, where it would eventually rescue Miller in the Thai fishing boat.

Cricket started to receive requests from the downed helicopters. Out of the initial assault, only one helicopter managed to return to Thailand. 7AF lost three choppers. K32 and JG41 made their run to the East Beach. They could see the smoke from the two helicopters on fire. K32, piloted by First Lieutenant Michael Lackey, approached the beach and received heavy machine-gun fire. An RPG struck the side of his helicopter; Lackey had to abort the mission. He flew across the neck of the island to the western side of Koh Tang. Fortunately, Lackey saw K21 in the water. He had to release fuel to

lighten the CH-53C, but he did manage to pick up Denham and the rest of the crew.

There were still four helicopters in the area. Lackey, in K32, still had his marines and was ready to try an insertion on the East Beach again. JG41 had just refueled from an HC-130P. Two other helicopters, JG42 and JG43, were minutes from their scheduled landing times. Cricket's controllers were getting overwhelmed with information and requests for support and instructions. McDaniel wanted Cricket to send in reinforcements, but the planned landings were in confusion. K32 started towards the East Beach, but Lackey saw the two helicopters on fire. He asked Cricket for instructions; the EC-130 controllers decided to move the force onto the West Beach area. The remaining helicopters followed K32 to the western beaches.

JG41 started to hover. Enemy fire scored direct hits on the right fuel tank and rear ramp area. First Lieutenant Thomas Cooper, the aircraft commander, decided to abort. JG42 and JG43 also tried to set down at about 0620hrs. First Lieutenant Phillip Pacini, JG42's pilot, identified two potential landing zones. These sites were north and south of the neck connecting the East and West Beaches. JG42 went to the southern site and found no marines. Captain Wayne Purser, in JG43, took the northern site. Purser's helicopter received small-arms fire. The Cambodian opposition proved too much. JG42 and JG43's pilots decided to try each other's location on the West Beach; they merely switched landing zones.

Lackey started his approach as he tried to reach McDaniel's position, but his helicopter was not immune to the intense ground fire. While trying to offload the marines, one of the helicopter's minigun operators was wounded. Denham and the rescued K21 crew had to endure another attack while the marines disgorged from K32. As soon as 13 marines offloaded about 0623hrs, Lackey rushed back to U-Tapao. One wounded marine and the Army linguist stayed aboard. Departing marines tried to get the linguist to move to the landing zone, but he refused to leave the helicopter. Under intense Khmer Rouge attack, the marines managed to leave K32. An A-7D flew overhead, but without a FAC marking enemy positions it couldn't attack, as the potential of hitting friendly forces was great. Furthermore, the Cambodians had advanced as close as 25yd to American positions. Despite the US aircrafts' ability to drop bombs and strafe accurately, the distance between the East and West Beaches was less than a mile, so a pilot aiming for one beach could hit the other with a misplaced bomb. A-7D pilots tried to fly low to get the Cambodians to fire on them and allow the airborne FAC to identify locations. The Khmer Rouge defenders, however, did not take the bait. Unfortunately, marines on the ground could not talk to the A-7Ds directly. Instead, they radioed Cricket, and the EC-130 passed requests for close air support to an orbiting A-7D FAC.

Lackey's CH-53C had suffered massive damage to the fuselage, many fuel leaks, and hydraulic problems from gunfire and a RPG round that actually went through the helicopter. He took the helicopter back to Thailand, but it was incapable of flying again.

Purser tried again. This time he selected a landing site south of the West Beach. Among a rocky patch, JG43 set down Austin, his command group,

OVERLEAF:

One of the most frustrating tasks that faced American forces during the Koh Tang operation was the rescue of K23's five crewmembers, Second Lieutenant Michael Cierce and 19 other marines, as the Khmer Rouge foiled several USAF extraction attempts. The men were under constant fire and the fears of the Khmer Rouge overrunning his position at night forced CINCPAC to attempt another extraction. At 1820hrs Cierce's men used an orange smoke marker to identify their position, while AC-130 gunships, F-4s, A-7Ds, OV-10As, and USAF helicopters provided suppressing fire. Fortunately, the extraction succeeded as JG11, a USAF HH-53C helicopter, rescued all from the East Beach by 1823hrs.

The 21st Special Operations Squadron AC-130Hs gave CINCPAC a unique ability to observe and fight the Cambodians. These Korat-based aircraft had a variety of weapons. Their 20mm guns allowed Air Force crews to destroy enemy positions or boats throughout the incident, day or night. (US Air Force)

OPPOSITE RIGHT: This series of AC-130 video stills shows JG13's attempt to rescue the K23 survivors on the East Beach. From top, JG13 approaches the landing zone; maneuvers to land with its rear cargo ramp toward the beach; then is hit by Cambodian defensive fire, igniting an external fuel tank and flare box. Finally, JG13 aborts the mission after a crew member dumps the flare box overboard. (US Air Force)

and a section of 81mm mortars. The location was isolated from McDaniel's position. Austin and the other 28 marines were assigned to support Company G's heavily armed infantry; his men did not have many M-16s. Austin's command group included radio operators, support staff, and the mortar men armed mostly with .45-caliber pistols and only four M-16s. If the Khmer Rouge attacked, they might not hold them back. Austin's group was about three-quarters of a mile south of the original landing zone.

Pacini, on his second try, placed his marines near McDaniel's position. Onboard JG42 was Company G's executive officer, First Lieutenant Dick Keith. Keith took command of the perimeter when he met McDaniel. Keith and McDaniel did not know if their company commander, Davis, was on the island. One of Keith's first directives was to knock out a Cambodian machine gun north of the landing site. Two marines did succeed in eliminating the gun position. Keith then planned a link-up with Austin.

Pacini's helicopter limped back to U-Tapao. The enemy fire had damaged the helicopter's flight control system and fuselage. JG42 had to refuel on its return to the base, since it had taken several hits on an external fuel tank. Pacini's helicopter would not fly again that day.

The Cambodian fire against Cicere's East Beach position intensified. At least the western side of the island had more marines; Cicere only had 25 men and some were wounded. Cricket controllers decided to pull out the marines and Air Force personnel. Fortunately, JG13, from the *Mayaguez* recovery effort, was orbiting the area and could try to extract everyone from the beach. A-7D strikes took out some Cambodian bunkers – First Lieutenant John Lucas, K23's co-pilot, had started to use his survival radio to identify enemy positions. As the situation unfolded, A-7D, AC-130, and F-4 pilots started to observe and attack the Cambodian locations. Lucas helped direct an AC-130 to fire ten 40mm rounds against the Khmer Rouge.

JG13 reached Cicere's position. As the helicopter positioned itself to take on the 25 survivors, the HH-53C was in the gun sights of machine guns, AK-47s, and other weapons. The rear ramp minigun swept the tree line, but the helicopter suffered multiple heavy automatic hits. Cicere was 75yd north of JG13 and could not move due to intense Cambodian opposition. JG13 had to break off the rescue attempt. Khmer Rouge soldiers had punctured an external fuel tank with machine-gun fire that ignited the tank. Fortunately, the flame-retardant system in the tank worked and the fuel did not explode. Inside JG13, the crew also had to jettison an ignited flare box. The flight control system, rotor hits, cockpit damage, and numerous leaks in the oil, fuel, and hydraulic lines forced the helicopter to creep back to U-Tapao. The HH-53C had to request aerial refueling because of the damaged external

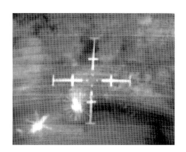

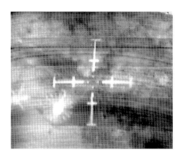

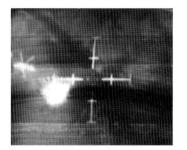

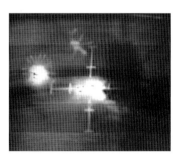

fuel tank; it made it back to Thailand, but had to land about 25 miles from U-Tapao. Another helicopter was inoperative for a second assault or rescue attempt.

JG41 was the last helicopter from the initial assault group. Cooper was still trying to land near Keith and McDaniel's position as the A-7D FAC tried to determine where the Khmer Rouge defenders had built their defending positions on the western beaches. JG41 had refueled and was ready to make another run. While waiting to launch their second landing, Cooper and First Lieutenant Dave Keith, his co-pilot, contacted the A-7D FAC to direct support for the marines. The FAC called on an AC-130H, Spectre 61, which could now help Cooper and Keith. Spectre 61 conducted fire-suppression attacks against Cambodian positions between the two marine positions on the western beaches. With A-7D and Spectre 61 help, Cooper tried to push on to the landing zone at 0835hrs, but enemy fire again repulsed JG41.

Cooper and Keith needed another refueling by an HC-130P. Despite extensive damage to their chopper, JG41 tried again at 0915hrs. In this attempt, Cooper flew towards the beach with its left minigun facing the beach to provide covering fire. The chopper suffered hits to its rotor blades and engine cowling. The third attempt at dropping off the marines was unsuccessful.

After receiving reports and observing fire from the Cambodians, Spectre 61 located enemy fortifications. The marines on the West Beach raised Spectre 61 and they fed reports of Cambodian locations at 0938hrs. The AC-130H aircraft used 14 105mm howitzer rounds to destroy some Khmer Rouge log bunkers north of the marine positions on the West Beach. The AC-130H crew also used 20mm and 40mm guns to sweep the targets. With this additional support and the destruction of the log fortifications, Cooper made another effort to drop off the marines.

At 1000hrs, JG41 made the run. This time, Cooper was able to drop off 20 marines under fire, but the Khmer Rouge started to ring the landing zone with mortar fire. As rounds moved closer to Cooper's helicopter – the Khmer

ABOVE LEFT: Air Force AC-130H crew members operate a 105mm howitzer. Crews used the 105mm howitzer to knock out several enemy fortified positions, including a log bunker that kept the western area marines from uniting. This aircraft type was so successful that it continues in use today. (US Air Force)

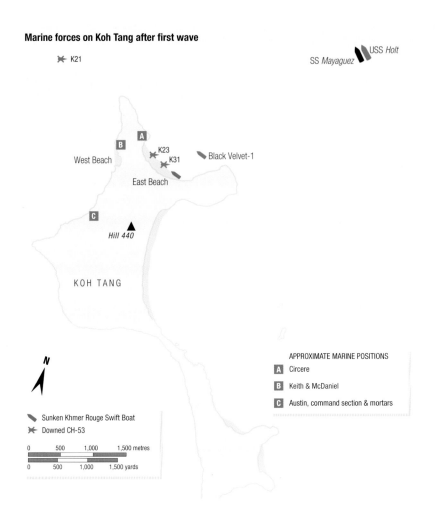

Marine forces on Koh Tang after first wave

K21

USS *Holt*

SS *Mayaguez*

A

B

K23

West Beach

K31

Black Velvet-1

East Beach

C

Hill 440

KOH TANG

N

APPROXIMATE MARINE POSITIONS

A Circere

B Keith & McDaniel

C Austin, command section & mortars

Sunken Khmer Rouge Swift Boat

Downed CH-53

| 0 | 500 | 1,000 | 1,500 metres |
| 0 | 500 | 1,000 | 1,500 yards |

Rouge mortar team landed one mortar round about 10ft from the tail rotor – he realized that he might have to leave immediately. Five marines remained on JG41. Cooper and Keith decided to make a fifth try at the landing zone. While JG41 hovered over the landing zone, mortar fire passed through the rotor and exploded 20ft from the helicopter. The chopper received more damage from mortar shrapnel. JG41 had to leave the area with the five marines to refuel. Despite their willingness to continue, Cooper received orders to abort and return to U-Tapao. If the Cambodians had shot down JG41, no helicopters were in the area to rescue them.

Austin tried to move north and meet up with Keith and McDaniel. Some marines from the West Beach enclave did advance south, but they encountered heavy opposition. Intense machine-gun fire and Claymore mines halted the attempt. One marine died and several others received wounds. Entrenched Cambodian defenders blocked the path. AC-130 20mm and 40mm gun operators sprayed the area. They tried to limit their gunfire to at least 150ft from friendly forces. Austin would try again later.

After Cooper left, 131 marines and five Air Force crew personnel held three positions on Koh Tang. The West Beach contained 82 marines. Austin's group, south of that position, had 29. Twenty-five other personnel hung on at the East Beach. CH-53C and HH-53C crew had planned on delivering 180 marines. The marines at U-Tapao waited for the second assault wave, but combat losses had decimated the helicopter force. Out of 11 helicopters used on the first wave, eight were either destroyed or suffered extensive damages beyond repair. Reinforcing the first wave of the marines would be difficult.

The second wave

Ford and the NSC knew that Miller and the *Mayaguez* crew were in American hands. Miller, his crew, and the team from the *Holt* rescue force had started to get the container ship underway. All seemed going as planned, except for the Koh Tang operation. With fewer forces on the ground, split up into three groups, facing more opposition than thought, and the possibility of enemy reinforcements, the marines were in a perilous situation. CINCPAC had scheduled the second wave to kick off at 1000hrs. Delays inserting the first wave and helicopter losses forced 7AF and Marine Corps officials to reassess the plan. The marines only had three helicopters left from the first assault. These helicopters were not the only ones in Thailand. Air Force maintenance crews had made two additional CH-53Cs operational and available for the second wave. K51 and K52 would now enter the fray. Five helicopters could now insert marines to protect the original wave from Khmer Rouge forces overruning them.

CINCPAC's original plan had scheduled upwards of 12 helicopters to emplace 250 marines and others to reinforce the initial assault. 7AF could not provide half of the choppers. The air support for Koh Tang also needed replacement. A-7D FACs had tried to operate through the confusion of the first wave – these aircraft pilots had trained with the 40th ARRS for rescue attempts, not providing ground support for marines. Fortunately, 7AF could call on the 23rd Tactical Air Support Squadron (TASS) at Nakhon Phanom. The 23rd TASS had first deployed to Thailand in 1966 and had remained in-theater. The squadron operated 40 OV-10As, and it had many combat FAC veterans using the call sign "Nail." The OV-10As were powered by twin propellers, which allowed them to maneuver at low speeds. Nail aircraft had extensive training in providing provide close air support missions. Compared to the A-7D, the two-man OV-10A crew had wider visibility and another set of eyes to direct ground-attack sorties. Four Nails moved from Nakhon Phanom to U-Tapao to support the second assault.

One of the major difficulties facing American military forces was the thick jungle terrain on Koh Tang. Finding and destroying the heavily defended areas or spotting moving Khmer Rouge was difficult due to the lush vegetation. This shot from a HH-53C demonstrates the problem for minigun operators. (US Air Force)

The Navy was also getting ready to support the Koh Tang operation. After the *Wilson* transferred Miller back to his ship, the missile destroyer could now use its twin 5in guns to attack island defenses. In addition, the *Coral Sea* moved closer to Koh Tang, which would allow Navy A-6As, A-7Es, and F-4Ns to conduct bombing and strafing missions against the Cambodians. Yet they never had the chance, since it would take too much time to coordinate strikes with the 7AF and solve communications problems. Air Force helicopters, however, could drop off wounded men and

K22 received severe damage that forced the crew to return to Thailand. They tried to make it to U-Tapao, but failed. The marines and Air Force crew left the CH-53C and later disabled the helicopter. Initially, the crew thought they had landed in Cambodia, as the helicopter's instrumentation had sustained damage. (US Air Force)

refuel faster by landing on the carrier deck rather than flying back to Thailand. Also, in the case of a possible evacuation, the CH-53C and HH-53C aircraft might have to drop off the marines on the *Coral Sea*. The carrier could make available two unarmed SH-3G rescue helicopters that might help with such an evacuation.

The Thai government was already complaining about the use of U-Tapao to attack Cambodia, and pressure mounted to stop operations from Thailand. Despite Thai protests, Burns had to launch a second wave of marines against Koh Tang. Five helicopters prepared to leave. The first pair, K52 and JG43, left U-Tapao about 0930hrs. Once refueled, JG11 and JG12 made their first attempt to hit Koh Tang when they departed at 1000hrs. K51 was last and it left at 1010hrs. The force contained 127 marines.

At about 1110hrs, Schlesinger ordered the marines on Koh Tang extracted with minimum casualties. The NMCC used a satellite communications system to beam a host of directives, orders, questions, and requests to CINCPAC, COMUSSAG/7AF, and Johnson, the marine ground force commander, at U-Tapao. Since the American military controlled the *Mayaguez* and her crew, further actions on Koh Tang seemed pointless. Instead of taking more casualties, JCS planners believed it was best to pull out of Koh Tang. However, the marines on Koh Tang needed help since the Khmer Rouge continued to attack their positions.

A JCS directive ordered CINCPAC to develop an extraction plan and explained that there was no reason to keep marines on the island or capture it. Later, the JCS amplified on the directive by telling CINCPAC not to send additional marines onto Koh Tang, but the second wave was already in the air and ready to hit the landing zones. Johnson was livid with the JCS directive. He asked how the helicopters could extract the marines if they had not even secured the landing zones. If CINCPAC followed the Ford and Schlesinger directives to the letter, then the Koh Tang marines would have to secure their defensive perimeters on their own. A second wave of marines could help secure the positions and allow for a safer extraction. Burns and the Commanding General, Fleet Marine Force Pacific, agreed and pressed the JCS to reconsider the order. Jones rescinded the order and allowed the second wave to continue. The NMCC and the JCS appeared not to have a full picture of the problems on Koh Tang.

While the second wave of helicopters headed to Koh Tang, Austin's group attempted to link up with Keith. Austin had an air liaison officer who managed to coordinate A-7D strikes, and he also used his 81mm mortar section to suppress the enemy. Spectre 61 had left to refuel in Thailand. The only remaining aircraft were A-7Ds and F-4s. Without proper marking smoke and landmarks, the marines used a radio to vector in the A-7Ds, which strafed the Khmer Rouge with their 20mm guns and dropped 500lb bombs. These attacks broke up the Cambodian defenders. Shortly before noon, just as the second wave approached the island, Austin reached his objectives on Keith's perimeter. On his route north, Austin's men saw a destroyed Khmer Rouge 106mm recoilless rifle.

First Lieutenant Robert E. Rakitis, K52's aircraft commander, made the first attempt to land on the East Beach. Despite many attempts from other helicopters and the loss of two craft, Cricket sent K23 in too. K51 and JG43 would follow. Rakitis immediately took heavy fire. Machine-gun rounds ripped open his fuel tanks. The pilot tried to cross the island to the West Beach, but fuel loss became critical. The CH-53C did not have a refueling boom, and the pilot had to abort rather than risk running out of fuel. His attempt to land marines failed. K51 and JG43 watched K52 abort. They moved across the island to land on the West Beach

K51 and JG43 tried to provide mutual minigun fire support to one another while they dropped off the marines. Khmer Rouge soldiers started to pepper the helicopters as they attempted to hover and discharge members of Company E. First Lieutenant Richard C. Brims, piloting K51, swept in first. The helicopter went to touch down on the beach several times. Eventually, Brims set down the CH-53C on the surf. The marines left, but Brims waited to receive five critically wounded. Remarkably, the CH-53C suffered only minor damage. Cambodian soldiers had let loose with small arms, grenades, and other weapons from positions about 150ft from the landing zone, but Brims returned to Thailand. JG43 also positioned itself for insertion. The HH-53C quickly discharged its marines without any serious problems. After leaving the beach, Purser, still piloting JG43, refueled from an HC-130P.

JG11 and JG12 arrived on the West Beach landing zone at about 1150hrs. The landing zone only had enough room for one helicopter, so the second helicopter provided minigun fire support to keep the Khmer Rouge from shooting down the other. The West Beach perimeter had continued to receive attention from Cambodian attacks. Fortunately, JG11 and JG12 offloaded their marines without serious incident. The arrival of additional marines was welcome. After JG12's marines left the helicopter, the chopper departed to Thailand with four wounded marines. JG11 also sought the HC-130P to get fuel.

The marines on Koh Tang still faced intense opposition. At least Austin had consolidated his position with Companies E and G. Davis, the Company G commander, had finally arrived on one of the helicopters in the second assault wave. There were now 226 Americans on Koh Tang. Austin had a force of 201 personnel on the West Beach and Cicere still held on with his group of 25. All of the groups were under intense fire, but the marines continued to hold back any opposition. The marines tried to expand their perimeters to

Marines leave K22 with their equipment. They did not land on Koh Tang, but had to return to Thailand. Unfortunately, the CH-53C was unable to land at U-Tapao since it had suffered extensive damage attempting to land on the West Beach. The marines returned to U-Tapao via JG12. (US Air Force)

This HH-53C, probably JG12, landed to take K22's crew and marines back to U-Tapao. JG12 had just delivered marines to the *Holt* to retake the *Mayaguez*. The helicopter was unscathed from enemy fire, unlike the initial wave of helicopters hitting Koh Tang. JG12 would later participate in combat actions at Koh Tang. (US Air Force)

**MAY 15
1975**

**1110hrs
Extraction order
given**

K23 lies on the East Beach, tail rotor shot off. Miraculously, no one died in the crash. The CH-53Cs were more vulnerable to enemy fire than the HH-53Cs, since they reduced armor and minigun protection for additional cargo capacity. The USAF lost five CH-53Cs in the mission. (US Air Force)

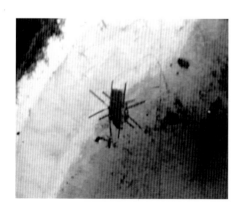

secure the western landing zone, but made little headway against the entrenched defenders and the jungle. The blistering firefights had forced the marines to expend their ammunition. Heat and humidity also took their toll, and the Americans started to run out of water. Austin could do little to rescue Cicere.

Two helicopters flew towards Thailand with wounded personnel. JG11 and JG43 had taken on JP-4 fuel and were ready to conduct rescue operations. K52 had suffered too much damage to return to Koh Tang. Extracting the marines out of Koh Tang would be a slow business, since there were only four helicopters left. Fortunately, the *Coral Sea* was now about 70 nautical miles from the island and closing. It could serve as a helicopter base. The *Wilson* was also offshore to provide naval gunfire support and could possibly pick up any survivors with Black Velvet-1 and a whaleboat.

The rescuers need rescue

Through the afternoon, the West Beach marines consolidated their positions and the defensive perimeter seemed secure, but the Cambodians could attack at any time. The marines and Navy corpsmen meanwhile kept watch for snipers and defended against probing Cambodian attacks. One group that needed rescue was the East Beach survivors. They had endured a helicopter crash, had seen unsuccessful attempts at reinforcement, and had witnessed JG13's failed rescue mission. Air Force CH-53C and HH-53C aircraft would lead the extraction effort. However, the Navy was also available to provide vital aid to the Americans on Koh Tang. The *Coral Sea* and the *Wilson* gave CINCPAC more flexible options to pull the Americans off the island.

After the *Wilson* had returned Miller to the *Mayaguez*, Commander J. Michael Rodgers, the guided-missile destroyer's captain, turned the ship towards Koh Tang. *Wilson* had saved one group of survivors earlier, extracting them from the West Beach. They would now act in another capacity. While Rodgers maneuvered past the northern tip of Koh Tang, a Khmer Rouge machine gun opened up on the

Wilson. The crew of the 5in gun returned fire and silenced the Cambodian position. Unfortunately, Rodgers had no detailed navigational charts to guide the ship. He managed to establish a cruising pattern offshore of the East Beach and cove. Staying within a six-fathom depth, Rodgers could provide gunfire support for the marines pinned down on the beach. The ship followed a pattern that allowed it to stay 1,000–3,000yds offshore at a speed of 3 knots, far enough away from shore to avoid RPG or heavy automatic fire. The *Wilson* did have problems, however, identifying targets. Without proper marking smoke or charts, plotting an accurate position for the two 5in guns proved difficult. Despite this problem, the *Wilson*'s crew and A-7D pilots worked together to locate positions, identify landmarks, and adjust fire to allow the gunners onboard to deliver deadly rounds. *Wilson* crew members identified hits on a chart and recorded their position for later references when firing their main gun batteries.

The *Wilson* added another dimension to the rescue. Its physical presence could intimidate the Cambodians, especially with her twin 5in guns. In addition, the ship's gig and whaleboat could help evacuate Cicere's marines and give another source of gunfire support by using Black Velvet-1. The ship also offered a stable platform to observe and spot enemy activity.

At 1430hrs, JG11 and JG43 began a run towards the East Beach. In this situation, Cricket directed A-7Ds to drop RCA munitions in the area. JG43 crew, wearing gas masks, would go in first while JG11 stood by with her miniguns. Unfortunately, the tear gas drifted offshore and was useless to JG43. One of the miniguns had also jammed. Purser, JG43's commander, decided to go into the area anyway. Enemy gunfire caused heavy damage to the fuel lines in the helicopter. Fuel sprayed throughout the cargo compartment and bullets cut a fuel line to an engine, crippling the helicopter. JG43 could not continue the rescue, but instead flew towards the *Coral Sea*. Purser managed to land his fuel-starved helicopter. Naval aircraft maintenance personnel and the Air Force flight mechanic on board replaced the damaged fuel line with rubber tubing and radiator clamps. JG11 had to abort too and it also landed on the *Coral Sea*.

Air Force maintenance crews in Thailand worked fast on damaged helicopters or those undergoing routine maintenance. By 1100hrs, they had made another HH-53C operational. JG44 would add a valuable resource to the limited helicopter pool.

The OV-10As had departed from Nakhon Phanom for U-Tapao and flew to the Koh Tang area to relieve the A-7D FACs. Nail-68, flown by Major Robert W. Undorf, and another OV-10A, Nail-47, arrived on station at about 1620hrs. Undorf took stock of the situation. He contacted the marines, the *Wilson*, Cricket, and Lucas, the co-pilot of K23 on the West Beach. Nail-68 was able to mark enemy positions with smoke rockets to help direct support fire from

**MAY 15
1975**

**2015hrs
Extraction
completed**

The BLU-82 was, at the time, the largest conventional bomb in the Air Force's inventory. It weighed 15,000lb, and engineers designed the aluminum powder bomb to clear helicopter landing zones during the Vietnam War. Delivered by a C-130, the bomb would create a 250ft diameter cleared area. (US Air Force)

This view from JG11 shows the short distance between the East and West Beach areas. The rear cargo ramp minigun allowed the Air Force crew to give covering fire to marines entering or exiting the helicopter. The six-barreled 7.62mm minigun was a potent weapon. (US Air Force)

aircraft and the *Wilson*. He also helped assess the situation to aid the marine evacuation from the West Beach. Discussion among all parties dismissed an option of using the *Wilson*'s armed gig and whaleboat to land near Cicere, since the boats could only carry 15 survivors at a time, and the Cambodians might overrun the diminishing number of defenders. However, Black Velvet-1 could stand offshore and the crew use its M-60s for suppressing fire against the Cambodians. The gig could also stand by to rescue any Americans shot down in helicopters.

Throughout the afternoon, the marines watched 7AF aircraft deliver ordnance against the Cambodian fortifications, but time was running out. Although the West Beach had received additional men and support, the East Beach marines might suffer defeat at any time. Soon, daylight would end. Someone had to make a decision. CINCPAC could withdraw the marines before dark with the four helicopters available, with maybe JG43 on the *Coral Sea*, or wait until the next day. The decision to stay or go fell on Undorf and Austin, since no guidance came forward from Cricket. Austin requested extraction before nightfall.

Extracting the marines under darkness and against heavy enemy opposition required careful coordination. The Air Force aircraft and the *Wilson* could provide fire support. After seeing the *Mayaguez* off, the *Holt* sped towards Koh Tang. The destroyer escort's 5in gun gave the marines additional fire support on the West Beach side. On-station AC-130s – Spectre 11, 21, and 22 – could use their infrared sensors and low-light level television system to track and attack any Khmer Rouge forces. The major problem was helicopter availability. The only 7AF choppers available included JG11, JG12, JG43, JG44, and K51. The *Coral Sea* also had two SH-3Gs that could help, but they were unarmored and unarmed. M-16-armed marines could stay onboard to give the SH-3Gs some defensive power, albeit limited.

The extraction phase would again start with an attempt to get K23's survivors out first. A partially submerged Cambodian Swift boat, in the East Beach area, had repeatedly interfered with efforts to rescue Cicere. A-7D pilots attacked the boat, but failed to stop its crew from emerging to fire its machine guns. The Swift boat had opened up with its .50-caliber machine guns against JG11 and JG43 on their mission to extract Cicere. The *Wilson*'s 5in guns now focused on this target at 1633hrs. After several shots, about six Cambodians left the boat. *Wilson*'s gunners destroyed the boat with 22 rounds. Rodgers' 5in guns also let loose 157 shells against the Khmer Rouge in support of the marines.

After coordinating the mission, extraction began with JG11. It had left the *Coral Sea* with the two SH-3Gs, and they were ready to start the rescue at 1635hrs. Nail-68 and -47 directed accurate fire on enemy positions around Cicere. First on scene were F-4s, which delivered strafing fire and Mk 82 laser-guided bombs under Undorf and his wingman's direction. Next, A-7Ds roared in and attacked the Cambodians. JG11 flew in to pick up the survivors on the East Beach. JG12 and K51 had the mission of providing minigun support. JG43 also launched from the aircraft carrier, ready to lend help. Black Velvet-1 stood offshore firing its M-60s to keep Cambodians from shooting down JG11. Spectre 11's crew had its weapons ready to fire.

Undorf directed JG11 in after the AC-130 hit the Khmer Rouge positions. The marines on the beach popped a smoke grenade, and JG11 landed at 1820hrs. Undorf, the *Wilson*'s gig, and the other helicopters used their machine guns to suppress Khmer Rouge fire. The marines conducted an orderly withdrawal, firing with their M-16s as they retreated. Three minutes later, with all survivors aboard, JG11 headed towards the *Coral Sea*.

After JG11 departed, a C-130 dropped a BLU-82 in the middle of the island. The order came from CINCPAC. Unfortunately, no one told the marines on the island, Undorf, or others. Marines saw the BLU-82 deploy on a pallet dropped with a parachute. Some of the marines thought it was supplies. The 15,000lb bomb fell about 1,000yd south of the marines' West Beach perimeter. Witnesses reported seeing a huge mushroom cloud over the area. CINCPAC's desire to drop the BLU-82 drop shocked the marines. If the intention of the bomb drop was to intimidate the Cambodians, then it did not stop the attacks on the marines. No further BLU-82s fell on Koh Tang.

Cricket directed JG12 to examine the K23 crash site. Reports of a survivor in the area had surfaced. Unfortunately, they were false. Cambodians zeroed in on the HH-53C when it approached the site. A crew member lowered a hoist to K23, but suffered wounds from gunfire. Since one of the miniguns ran out of ammunition, JG12 had to maneuver the craft to allow one of her other weapons to shoot. Crew members also used small arms to fire from the windows. Undorf guided fire from K51 that stopped six Cambodian soldiers. JG12 then left, and the helicopter had to make a landing on the *Coral Sea* with damaged main and tail rotors, hydraulic lines, and fuel tanks. JG11 and JG12's ability to support further operations seemed questionable.

One of major problems facing Austin was communications difficulties. Undorf lost contact with Cricket. He did advise Austin about the helicopter extractions, but was not sure of the timing. The *Holt* could provide general assistance and Black Velvet-1 had moved from the eastern to the western side of the island.

Darkness was rapidly descending on the island. Cricket tapped K51 to lead the first run to Austin's position and try to pull out as many marines as possible. K51, along with JG43 and JG44, had orbited the West Beach. Smoke, haze, and the darkness made landing difficult. K51 would have to find the beach and hopefully discover the marines ready to withdraw quickly. At 1840hrs, K51 went in. The Khmer Rouge immediately opened fire and exchanged grenades with the marines, and the Cambodians used flares to illuminate the area. Fortuitously, the marines were ready to depart despite K51's surprise arrival. Navy corpsmen loaded the wounded into the chopper. K51 left, with 41 marines, for the *Coral Sea*.

CINCPAC ordered a C-130 to drop a BLU-82 on Koh Tang. This image shows the result of the 15,000lb bomb exploding. Deployed without warning, the resulting explosion surprised American as well as Cambodians. Marines on the *Holt* witnessed a shock wave passing over the island as a result. (US Air Force)

OPERATIONS AGAINST SS *MAYAGUEZ* AND KOH TANG

MAYAGUEZ LOCATIONS **1 – 11**
12–15 May

1 *Mayaguez* captured at 1420hrs on May 12.

2 *Mayaguez* anchors overnight at Poulo Wai due to a damaged radar.

3 *Mayaguez* seen heading north towards Kompong Som.

4 *Mayaguez* diverts to Koh Tang at 1325hrs on May 13 and remains overnight.

5 *Mayaguez* crew placed on Thai fishing boat on the morning of May 14. US aircraft fail to stop the boat and her escorts.

6 *Mayaguez* crew arrives at Kompong Som harbor at 0948hrs on May 14, but are refused entry.

7 *Mayaguez* crew moved to Koh Rong Sam Lem naval compound. Phnom Penh decides to release the crew, but they stay the night and depart at 0729hrs on May 15.

8 Thai fishing boat with Mayaguez crew seen heading to Koh Tang at 0935hrs.

9 USS Wilson intercepts the Thai fishing boat at 1008hrs.

10 Crew returns to *Mayaguez* at 1205hrs.

CARRIER STRIKE BY USS *CORAL SEA* **1 – 4**
May 15

1 0705hrs: Armed reconnaissance mission. The mission is cancelled and the aircraft are recovered at 0830hrs. A refinery north of Kompong Som is identified.

2 0845hrs: Strike mission against Ream airfield. Three Cambodian aircraft destroyed and several structures damaged.

3 1020hrs: Mission against Kompong Som area and Phumi Phsar naval base.

4 1155hrs: Launch of fourth mission cancelled.

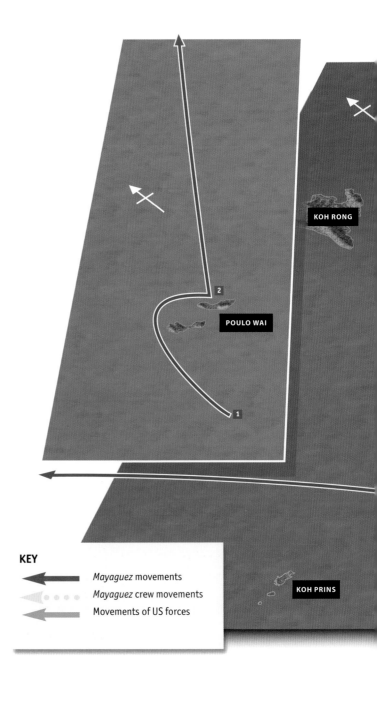

KOH RONG

2

POULO WAI

1

KOH PRINS

KEY

⬅ *Mayaguez* movements

◅ ● ● ● ● *Mayaguez* crew movements

◅ Movements of US forces

KOH TANG EXTRACTION

1 – 4   May 15

1 JG11 and JG43 fail to extract K23 survivors at 1430hrs.

2 JG11, with support from JG12, K41, JG44, Spectre 11, A-7Ds, F-4s, USS *Wilson*, and other forces rescues K23 survivors at 1820hrs.

3 C-130 drops a BLU-82 on Koh Tang shortly after the JG11 rescue.

4 Starting at 1840hrs, K51 rescues 41 marines on West Beach. JG43, JG44, and K51 (after returning from USS *Coral Sea*) recover the remaining marines. K51 is the last to leave at 2000hrs.

KOH TANG ISLAND ASSAULT

1 – 5   May 15

1 0415hrs: 11 CH-53C and HH-53Cs depart U-Tapao for Koh Tang and USS *Holt*.

2 0603hrs: K21 and K22 approach West Beach. K21 deploys marines, but takes fire and crashes in the sea. K22 aborts and is forced to land in Thailand.

3 K23 and K31 try to land on East Beach. K23 deploys marines and is shot down. K31 is destroyed by gunfire. K32 aborts and rescues the K21 crew, deploying marines in the west of the island. JG41 aborts, but tries repeatedly to land marines on West Beach. JG42 and JG43 land on West Beach.

4 JG11, JG12, and JG13 deliver marines to *Holt*.

5 *Mayaguez* is boarded and secured by 0822hrs.

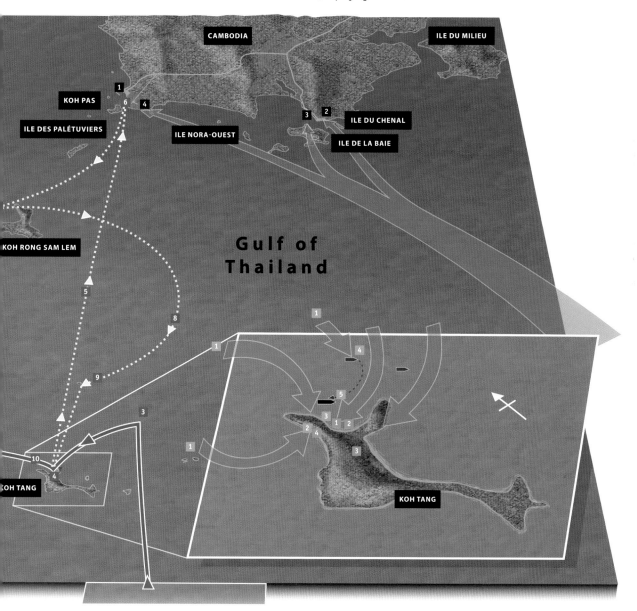

Next in line was JG43. Khmer Rouge small-arms and mortar fire erupted along the perimeter. Unfortunately, Undorf could not provide tactical jet or AC-130 suppressing fire in time. The OV-10s did mark enemy positions with smoke rockets, but in the darkness the A-7Ds would have a problem seeing the smoke. Purser had to provide whatever support from his miniguns and crew members with small arms. He landed seven minutes after K51's departure. JG43 had problems with its lighting system – the marines could only hear the helicopter – but they did manage to find the helicopter and start boarding. JG44 almost hit the blacked-out helicopter, when it tried to land in the same area. Fortunately, Purser had determined through radio transmissions that JG44 was inbound. He turned on his helicopter's searchlight to avoid a collision. Some 54 marines loaded on the HH-53C and Purser headed for the *Coral Sea* at 1850hrs. His chopper had suffered damage to his main rotor spar.

JG44 attempted another landing, but he had to abort again due to intense ground fire from the Cambodians. Its third try worked, and marines scrambled aboard at 1854hrs. The marines reported that they had moved the perimeter to about 50yd from the landing zone. JG44's crew was concerned that any return fire from their miniguns could hit the marines. With 40 marines onboard, the helicopter left for the *Holt* instead of the *Coral Sea*. JG44's lights were also not working, so a crew member vectored in the helicopter to the ship's landing pad by hanging outside of the chopper. After unloading the marines, JG44 went back to get more.

There were 73 marines left on the island. The biggest challenge was to ensure the Cambodians would not overrun the last US troops. Undorf and his wingman also returned to U-Tapao and another OV-10A pair replaced them. Spectre 21 had taken over from Spectre 11 and knocked out a mortar position. At 1915hrs, JG44 landed again with the aid of a strobe light thrown on the beach by Davis. The helicopter picked up 34 more men and had to land on the *Coral Sea* due to an engine problem.

Spectre 11 and the OV-10As kept the enemy at bay, since they were now the only aircraft available. K51 would have to take the last marines out alone, with the only minigun support coming from its two onboard weapons. Facing heavy opposition, K51 landed after four attempts. Under fire, poor lighting, and some confusion, the remaining marines executed their withdrawal and hurried aboard. The helicopter was ready to leave, but Technical Sergeant Wayne Fisk, a K51 crew member, left to search the area and make sure no one was left behind. Fisk looked around the tree line frantically while under fire. He found two marines still providing covering fire against the Khmer Rouge. All three returned to K51 with the helicopter leaving for the *Coral Sea* at 2015hrs, ending the 14-hour mission on Koh Tang.

With the evacuation complete, the rescue of the *Mayaguez* concluded. The mission cost 11 marines, two Navy corpsmen, and two Air Force crew members, with another 50 US troops wounded. There were also the 23 USAF personnel killed in the helicopter crash in Thailand. Cambodian casualties are unknown. Despite the efforts to withdraw carefully, three marines were left behind. The Cambodians later found and executed them, two of them at Kompong Som.

ANALYSIS

The *Mayaguez* incident had profound military implications. Ford and the NSC avoided another USS *Pueblo* incident, with its lengthy negotiations, and America certainly acted to defend its interests. Yet although successful in meeting the national objective of quickly securing the safe return of ship and crew, the mission provided sobering lessons that affect military activities today.

The *Mayaguez*'s legacy

Many aspects of the operation provided an early demonstration of modern communications advances. Despite the global distances, local commanders were now under the constant watch of their chain of command, from the President to their immediate headquarters. Commanders could now listen in, comment on, and override decisions by their field subordinates. The President could literally micro-manage a tactical situation instead of focusing on a strategic or long-term view. A local commander's initiative and ability to make decisions was therefore at risk of disappearing. Potentially, an organization in combat might suffer a loss of unity of command, as decisions from outside the immediate unit create confusion in direction, especially if leaders make those decisions with incomplete information or a lack of situational awareness. In addition, local commanders might have to wait for a decision, the loss of tempo destroying initiative and innovation. Communications and information technology improved dramatically after 1975. One might argue that the ability of high-level commanders to

In the photograph taken from JG11, the survivors from K23 scramble onboard the HH-53C. After several attempts to extricate Cicere's marines, the Air Force finally got the men off the East Beach. Fears of the marines' position being overrun by the Khmer Rouge made their rescue a priority over other rescues. (US Air Force)

affect tactical operations reached a critical juncture five years later during Operation *Eagle Claw*, which ended in a humiliating failure for forces trying to rescue American embassy hostages in Iran.

Presidential decision-making was also crucial to the incident. Ford had inherited the remains of the Vietnam conflict with Operation *Eagle Pull* and *Frequent Wind*. Finding some way to salvage America's honor by demonstrating that it was not a "paper tiger" would go a long way to sooth the pain of Vietnam. Some of NSC staff also wanted to avoid another USS *Pueblo* incident, which forced the nation into a bitter negotiation with the North Koreans. Under crisis, Ford and the NSC had to make decisions from 11 time zones away, and in some cases without benefit of current information. The ability to issue directives instantly to the field compounded this problem.

In some situations, rapid communications to direct subordinates is a definite advantage, assuming higher headquarters have all the available information. In the case of the *Mayaguez*, Ford's decision to cease all military operations and disengage with the Cambodians almost created a situation in which the extraction of the marines might have been bloodier. The choice to sink all boats in the Koh Tang area could also have resulted in the death of Miller and his crew on the Thai fishing boat, if not for the P-3 and the *Wilson*'s captain identifying Miller before firing. Without proper situational awareness by higher command, policies might be contradictory at best or deadly at worst.

Like many military operations, current and accurate information was lacking. CINCPAC forces did not have maps with the proper scale or accuracy to conduct targeting. More serious was the problem concerning enemy force estimates on Koh Tang. The three sources concerning enemy strength varied widely in their data. Intelligence reporting to the marines and 7AF units also seemed fragmented. Some received DIA/IPAC reports; the marines thought they would face limited opposition. Most military leaders would have planned for the worst, by using the DIA estimate of 150 to 200 Khmer Rouge soldiers. Similarly, if CINCPAC had an accurate location for the *Mayaguez* crew, then the Koh Tang assault might not have happened. CINCPAC did make corrections to intelligence dissemination and feedback based on its experience of the operation.

The various military forces used in the operation worked well together given the circumstances. Still, a lack of joint training affected their ability to operate together. Coordinating close air support between Air Force and USMC air units was difficult given their different communications systems. The capacity for Air Force helicopters to conduct a beach assault was also a challenge. Three downed and many damaged helicopters seriously impaired commanders' options for conducting a second-wave attack and extraction. However, the disparate forces were able to adapt and adjust to the difficult situation. Commanders also demonstrated flexibility in creating plans and conducting operations with the limited resources deployed in Southeast Asia. Washington pulled together and massed forces within hours of the *Mayaguez*'s capture. CINCPAC planners had to coordinate operations over wide geographic distances, and at great speed. Such missions, and problems encountered in Vietnam, Iran, and Grenada, led to more emphasis on inter-service cooperation, planning, training, and equipment. The Goldwater–Nichols Act of 1986 tried to address many of the issues about operating in a joint service environment and made significant progress in improving military capability.

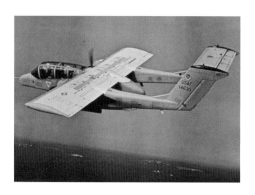

OV-10As, like this aircraft, from the 23rd Tactical Air Support Squadron took over forward air control duties from the 3rd Tactical Fighter Squadron A-7Ds. The OV-10As gave the marines and the aircrew crews a different perspective to control and direct operations against the Khmer Rouge. They worked in pairs: one briefed incoming aircraft, the other directed air strikes and kept watch over the area. (US Air Force)

Diplomatic moves at the time were particularly difficult to make given the recent Cambodian revolution. Washington attempted, through several avenues, to send messages to Phnom Penh to release the *Mayaguez*. Trying to establish who decided to seize and keep the crew has never been determined. State Department officials did not know whom to contact. They tried to get the Chinese government to intercede, initially unsuccessfully, but word eventually arrived from Tehran that a PRC diplomat indicated a release was possible. Time urgency and other motivations may have scuttled the White House's attempts to secure the release of the crew without having to initiate the Koh Tang operations. Diplomatic efforts take time, Ford and the NSC wanted to resolve the issue immediately.

During the *Mayaguez* incident, objectives and priorities seemed to be in conflict in some instances. The overall safety of the *Mayaguez* crew was potentially jeopardized by several actions, such as the sinking of patrol boats that might have held the captives, conducting air strikes near Kompong Som and Ream, and landing on Koh Tang without knowledge of the prisoners' location. Although CINCPAC and JCS planners designed the air raids on the Kompong Som area to avoid Cambodian reinforcements deploying to Koh Tang, the attacks they could have also worked against Washington. The original plan to use B-52s could have inflicted massive civilian casualties, turning world and domestic sympathy into condemnation. National leaders debated the use of the air raids: a demonstrative action or tactical support for the Koh Tang assault? Expanded American military actions throughout the region might have hardened Phnom Penh's stance on releasing the crew. Still, American air operations, including sinking Cambodian patrol boats, caught Phnom Penh's attention and played a significant part in the release of the *Mayaguez*'s crew.

A significant issue raised by the crisis was the question of when to use military force. Ford and the NSC first attempted diplomatic means of resolution, but unfortunately time demands and the desire to demonstrate America's military muscle may have short-circuited diplomacy. Trying to contact the Cambodian government directly was difficult, if not impossible. Without the ability to transmit American demands, Washington had to use third parties or the world press. This situation contributed to uncertainty about possible settlement of the crisis. Today, governments have similar problems contacting insurgents or other non-state actors, decreasing the likelihood of negotiated settlements and increasing the possibility of armed conflict.

Domestic political concerns also clouded the NSC's decision-making processes by creating an artificial time constraint. The War Powers Resolution and the Cooper–Church Amendment forced Ford to get the

Khmer Rouge defenders fought to stop all the Air Force rescue efforts. An A-7D aircraft dropped riot control agent cluster bombs on the East Beach in an attempt to suppress the Cambodians, but the wind blew the gas offshore into the helicopters instead. (US Air Force)

mission planned and completed before any serious congressional opposition developed. If the operation dragged on and incurred heavy casualties, the American public and Congress might have demanded a halt. CINCPAC had to plan and execute based on assumptions that Ford could convince Congress that the operation was necessary.

Some critics of the *Mayaguez* operation would argue that the loss of 41 American military personnel was too high to rescue the 40-member container ship crew. A simple cost analysis appears too simplistic. Indeed, larger national interests and objectives were at play above and beyond the release of crew and ship. The USMC, USAF, and US Navy personnel involved in the military operations in the Gulf of Thailand largely achieved all American mission objectives, but the toll was heavy.

The United States' image and credibility had suffered amongst her NATO allies and Cold War foes after Vietnam. The *Mayaguez* incident was a test of Washington's will and capability to use military force. The United States demonstrated that it would protect American interests globally. North Korea, the Soviet Union, China, and others watched as the nation reacted quickly and adapted to a dynamic situation. American military actions appeared to salvage the nation's honor and reputation abroad, but also domestically. By 1975, the United States had endured the loss of Vietnam, impeachment efforts and the resignation of a President, rising unemployment, and other problems. Despite the rescue of the *Mayaguez* and its crew, critics argued that the operation had several deadly flaws. Difficultes with joint planning, command and control, incompatibility of equipment, the War Powers Resolution, and operational mistakes resulted in congressional investigations and internal reviews within the Pentagon. Many of these difficulties, along with problems during the failed Iranian hostage rescue and Grenada operations, resulted in a movement to reform how Washington would conduct future joint operations, training, and acquisition of common equipment that would result in the Goldwater–Nichols Act of 1986, a major milestone in changing the face of the American military.

National leaders and the future

The national and military leaders involved in the *Mayaguez* incident went on to take very different paths. Gerald Ford survived the incident with a boost in his domestic popularity. He later reorganized his cabinet in a major shakeup in November 1975, known as the "Halloween Massacre." The cabinet became more conservative, and Ford replaced Kissinger for Scowcroft as his national security advisor. Still smarting from perceived problems in military planning, capability, and operations, Ford fired Schlesinger and replaced him with Donald Rumsfeld, the youngest Secretary

This photograph illustrates damage to JG13 after its failed attempt to land on the East Beach. A round entered the pilot's instrument panel via the lower windshield. JG13 was still able to fly, but was out of commission after the operation. (US Air Force)

of Defense. Rumsfeld's deputy, Richard Cheney, became Ford's White House Chief of Staff. George H. W. Bush became DCI when Ford forced Colby out. Bush would become the 41st President and Cheney served him as his Secretary of Defense. Coincidentally, Bush's son, George W. Bush, would become the 43rd President. He selected Cheney as his Vice President and Rumsfeld as Secretary of Defense. Several of these selections would have a significant impact on future American foreign policy. Unfortunately, Gerald Ford's later tenure suffered from declining presidential power, a very weak economy, and public resentment of his pardon of Richard Nixon. Although surviving two assassination attempts, Ford was not re-elected President. He died on December 26, 2006.

Henry Kissinger remained Secretary of State in the Ford administration. He retained great influence in foreign policy after he left office. As a scholar and consultant, Kissinger advised George W. Bush on a range of foreign policy issues, especially on Israel and the Middle East.

David C. Jones, then acting Chairman of the JCS, completed his tour as Air Force Chief of Staff. Jones rose to Chairman of the JCS in 1978. Jones had heavily criticized the planning and conduct of the *Mayaguez* incident. His solution was more intensively centralized command, control, and planning of similar military operations. Jones remained in office until 1982, when he retired. During his tenure, he oversaw the failed attempt to rescue American military and embassy personnel in Iran through Operation *Eagle Claw*, an action that suffered from constant micro-management from senior leadership.

CONCLUSION

Despite America's success in recovering the *Mayaguez*, Cambodia remained governed by one of the most murderous regimes in mankind's history. Pol Pot, the Khmer Rouge leader, consolidated his power after taking Phnom Penh on April 17, 1975. His agrarian revolution, which forced hundreds of thousands of urban dwellers into the fields, is infamous. Under his regime, 20–25 percent of the population perished due to starvation, overwork, or mass execution. Opposition to the Khmer Rouge grew, until Vietnam invaded in 1978 and replaced the government. Pol Pot himself died in 1998 while under house arrest.

American military actions did not sway Pol Pot into transforming his country into the "killing fields," nor did Cambodia slow its desire to extend territorial sovereignty over border regions and several islands in the Gulf of Thailand. American military operations did, however, weaken the Khmer

These F-4Ds from the 432nd Tactical Fighter Wing strafed and bombed Cambodian forces on Koh Tang and the Gulf of Thailand. Despite the protests and warnings from Bangkok, Washington used Thai-based aircraft and marines deployed from U-Tapao. (US Air Force)

Rouge in the region in May 1975, allowing the Vietnamese to increase their influence in the area. By June 1975, the Vietnamese had occupied Poulo Wai. The issue over borders created problems between Cambodia and her neighbors. One might argue that the mass exterminations and the border issues caused the Vietnamese to embark on a slow path to war with Cambodia, a journey that would eventually overthrow the Khmer Rouge.

The *Mayaguez* incident forced many to pause and think about Washington's response. Questions about the proportionality of response, executive branch decision-making, diplomatic versus military options, intelligence gathering, command and control, and concerns about military capability arose after the crisis. Modern technology had also altered the face of military operations for Washington.

Still, American military forces demonstrated their ability to conduct a rapid-response mission. Adaptive, creative leadership, along with valor, turned a potential disaster at Koh Tang into a successful evacuation. All services involved showed an ability to work out problems in spite of conflicting directives caused by higher officials unaware of the full situation. Hasty decisions and the ability to oversee and overturn a subordinate commander's decisions immediately could have seriously impaired the mission. Fortunately, Washington did allow local forces to operate with some flexibility. Future command and control, however, may have tighter reins and may influence events at even lower "tactical" levels than occurred in the *Mayaguez* incident. Communications technology has improved significantly and the sensitivity regarding collateral damage has only increased since 1975. The media is global and the damage done to a nation's image can, in some cases, be hurt more by a picture than actual combat operations.

The mission ultimately proved a success, but the loss of personnel and equipment was costly. Yet how does a nation balance the bill to implement national policy? Piracy, terrorism, hostage-taking, and other activities threaten a nation's ability to protect its citizenry and property aboard. Although missions like the *Mayaguez* seemed costly, what would Washington have had to pay for future events in the Gulf of Thailand and beyond if Ford did not stand up to Cambodia? The speed and use of force, which included attacks on Cambodia, underscored Washington's ability to respond to a crisis situation. Unfortunately for Washington, national leaders would have to prove this point on more than one occasion in the future.

Men of 2/9 Marines, Companies E and G, depart from the USS *Coral Sea*, after they left Koh Tang via Air Force helicopters. These marines were landed on the *Coral Sea* by crews of the 40th Aerospace Rescue and Recovery Squadron and 21st Special Operations Squadron. They returned to Subic Bay, the Philippines. (US Navy)

BIBLIOGRAPHY

Command History Branch, *Commander in Chief Pacific Command History 1975 Appendix VI – The SS Mayaguez Incident* (Top Secret), Camp Smith, HI, Office of the Joint Secretary (1976) (Declassified)

General Accounting Office, *The Seizure of the Mayaguez – A Case Study of Crisis Management*, Washington, DC, Comptroller General of the United States (1976)

Guilmartin, John F., Jr., *A Very Short War: The Mayaguez and the Battle of Koh Tang*, College Station, TX, Texas A&M University Press (1995)

Head, Richard G., et al., *Crisis Resolution: Presidential Decision Making in the Mayaguez and Korean Confrontations*, Boulder, CO, Westview Press (1978)

Johnson, Thomas R., *(U) American Cryptology during the Cold War, 1945–1989 (U) Book III: Retrenchment and Reform, 1972–1980* (Top Secret), CCH-S54-98-01, Fort Meade, MD, Center for Cryptologic History, National Security Agency (1998) (Declassified)

Joint Chiefs of Staff, *After Action Report US Military Operations SS Mayaguez/Kaoh Tang Island 12–15 May 1975* (Secret), Washington, DC, Office of Joint Chiefs of Staff (undated) (Declassified)

Joint Secretariat, *Note to the Joint Chiefs of Staff on The Rescue of the "SS Mayaguez" and its Crew (U)* (Secret), Washington, DC, Office of the Joint Chiefs of Staff (May 19, 1975) (Declassified)

Lamb, Christopher Jon, *Belief Systems and Decision Making in the Mayaguez Crisis*, Gainsville, FL, University of Florida Press (1989)

Messengee, J.A. et al, *"'Mayday' for the Mayaguez,"* *Naval Institute Proceedings* (November 1976)

Lavelle, A.C.J. (ed.), *The Vietnamese Air Force, 1951–1975: An Analysis of its Role in Combat and Fourteen Hours at Koh Tang*, Washington, DC, Office of Air Force History (1985)

Office of the Historian, *History of the Pacific Air Forces 1 Jul 74–31 Dec 75* (Secret), Hickam AFB, HI, CINCPACAF/HO (1976) (Declassified)

Major R.E. Porter (left) and Captain Walt Wood (right) raise the colors on the *Mayaguez* after its boarding. Wood's Company D, support personnel, explosive ordnance disposal team, and others searched the ship. They later helped get the ship ready to steam on her own, once the *Wilson* returned Miller to his ship. (US Navy)

Office of the Secretary of Defense, *Memorandum For the President Subject: Seizure of U.S. Ship Mayaguez* (Top Secret), Washington, DC, Office of the Secretary of Defense (undated) (Declassified)

Rowan, Roy, *The Four Days of Mayaguez*, New York, W. W. Norton (1975)

Wetterhahn, Ralph, *The Last Battle: The Mayaguez Incident and the End of the Vietnam War*, New York, Carroll & Graf (2001)

White House, *Memorandum of Conversation Subject: Mayaguez* (Secret), Washington, DC, Office of the President (May 14, 1975) (Declassified)

White House, *Minutes National Security Council Meeting Subject: Seizure of American Ship by Cambodian Authorities* (Top Secret/Sensitive), Washington, DC, Office of the President (May 13–15, 1975) (Declassified)

INDEX